PETER H

A YEAR GONE BY
A YORKSHIRE TOWN 1871

LOWNDES
PUBLICATIONS
(DRIFFIELD)

Published 1991

Lowndes Publications (Driffield)
17 Lowndes Park
Driffield
YO25 7BE

ISBN 0 9517630 0 8

A CIP catalogue record for this book
is available from the British Library.

CONTENTS

LIST OF ILLUSTRATIONS

The photograph on the cover is of Middle Street in Driffield and was taken between 1861 and 1871.

Acknowledgements

This study makes use of a wide variety of contemporary sources, particularly the Driffield Times and the Driffield Observer, (from which most of the quotations are taken), and the 1871 census. It would be tedious, indeed pretentious, in a work of this nature to overburden the text with references. I have therefore adopted the practice of giving the source of quotations only when they are not from the two newspapers, or where it is not obvious from the text which source has been used.

The Driffield Times for 1871 is kept in the Newspaper Offices and I am grateful to the Editor and staff for their unfailing patience in putting up with me as a frequent visitor. The illustrations on pages 7, 12, 49, 69, 73 and 89 are produced with the permission of the Driffield Times.

The Driffield Observer for 1871, to the best of my knowledge, is not available locally, but copies exist in the British Newspaper Library in London. The illustrations on pages 23 and page 36 are reproduced by permission of the British Library.

No copies of the Driffield Express have survived for 1871 --- always a dangerous statement to make about Driffield !

The engraving of the Driffield Pure Linseed Cake Company on page 34, is taken from Jarratt's pamphlet on the linseed trade and is reproduced, with permission, from the Local History collection of Humberside Library.

The photograph of Middle Street, used on the cover, is reproduced by permission of Barclays Bank.

My thanks are also due to the staff of the Humberside County Record Office in Beverley, for their help and courtesy.

Peter Howorth
February 1991

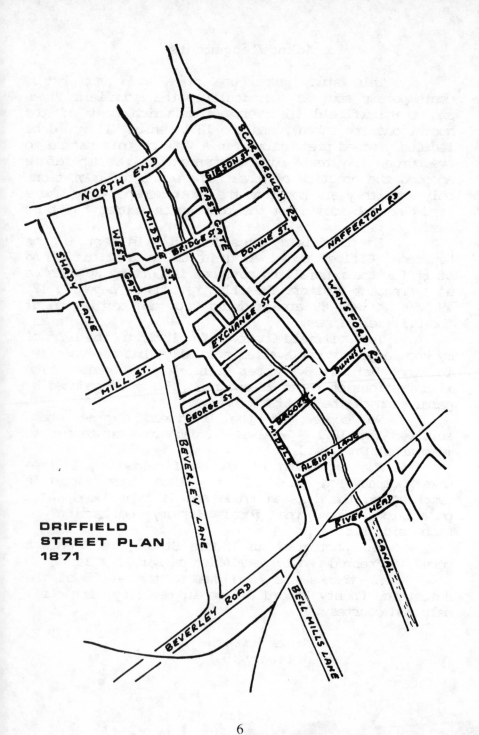

DRIFFIELD
STREET PLAN
1871

NORTH END
SCARBOROUGH RD
GIBSON ST.
EAST GATE
WEST GATE
MIDDLE ST.
BRIDGE ST.
SHADY LANE
DOWNE ST.
NAFFERTON RD
WANSFORD RD
EXCHANGE ST
MILL ST.
GEORGE ST.
BROOKS.
MIDDLE ST.
ALBION LANE
DUNNIL
BEVERLEY LANE
RIVER HEAD
CANAL
BEVERLEY ROAD
BELL MILLS LANE

6

CHAPTER ONE

JANUARY

The winter of 1870-71 was severe. The last three months of 1870 had seen sixty-two wet days and half the year's rainfall (13.56"). The harvest had been an early one which meant that in the "long black end of the year" work was scarce for the many day labourers seeking employment. By January the snow was heavy enough for sleighs to become the fashion and for the local papers to complain of "hair breadth escapes" by pedestrians from the speeding horses.Christmas hampers were still being advertised as containing "six bottles of best wines and spirits (one brandy, port, sherry, gin, rum and whiskey) for 22/-" but it was pointed out in the Driffield Times that in "the intensely cold stern winter" work was scarce, most kinds of provisions were dear and the poor were in need of a soup kitchen.The landlord of the Buck responded and agreed to supply once a week, a quart of soup to the deserving poor for the next four weeks.

At Westminster the Liberal government, secure with a 112 majority, followed its programme of domestic reforms.Gladstone, elected Prime Minister for the first time in 1868, was at 61 (in 1871) at his most energetic.Already on the statute books were acts disestablishing the Irish Church, protecting Irish tenants and reforming the English education system. Major reforms of the universities, the civil service, trade unions and the army were proceeding. Cardwell's army reforms were made all the more urgent by events in France. At a time when an expeditionary force of 10,000 was the largest that the War Office could contemplate, Prussia and her allies employed an army of 475,000 in the initial stages of the Franco-Prussian war.

Driffield people followed the speedy defeat of the French armies, the capture of Napoleon III and the I3I day siege of Paris in the town's three newspapers. In the understandable absence of a reporter in Paris, the Driffield Times reprinted reports of events from the Daily Telegraph and the Yorkshire Post. Public opinion, as expressed in these articles, was pro-French. In the January 7th paper, Driffield read of Prussian "atrocities" committed on Christmas Day. The Bishop of Versailles' appeal for the starving in Paris was reported on the 14th. The shelling of Paris, which began on January 5th was reported sixteen days later and the surrender of Paris on January 27th was reported by the Driffield Times on February 4th with "almost unbelief". France had been "subdued by a higher military culture and a stronger military civilisation". The Driffield Observer gave much fuller reports on both the war and other foreign news, usually reporting events in France some seven days after they happened. No copies of the Driffield Express have survived for the period.

The three Driffield papers were weekly ones. Later in the year, Holderness, the proprietor of the Driffield Observer, started to receive a supply of the York Herald off the Malton train every Friday evening and delivered them the same night to people who had ordered them. Those people who had access to the regional and national papers would have earlier knowledge of events. This would include in Driffield, members of the Mechanics' Institute who subscribed to newspapers and periodicals for their Reading Room. G.R.Jackson sold "photographs of all the principal personages of the Franco-Prussian war" at 6d each in his shop and East Riding farmers launched an appeal for seed to supply French farmers.

The long winter evenings were the season for social events and for meetings of the town's societies. The Driffield and East Riding Agricultural Society held their annual general meeting, as did the Driffield Mechanics' and Literary Institute in their rooms above Exchange Street. They reported that 6114 volumes had been issued to the 200 members who also had access to the Reading Rooms. The prestigious offices in the Institute were held by leading figures in the town. A local industrialist, Francis Matthews, took over the Presidency from George Hodgson, a solicitor. The two Vice-Presidents were the artist, Alexander Lydon and Henry Marshall, who owned King's Mill.The eight man committee was filled by small tradesmen alongside one or two young men who were making their mark in local society such as the ambitious Luke White. The programme of lectures, literary and musical entertainments were very popular. The Rev. W. Mitchell's lecture on "The Two Napoleons: a comparison and a contrast" may have helped local understanding of the situation in France and Ross lectured on "Physics, metallurgy and toxicology", but the most crowded meetings were the programme of penny readings by local personalities which attracted omnibus parties from the surrounding villages and which sometimes had to turn away people.

The other main social venues in the town were the Corn Exchange and the Assembly Rooms on Bridge St., where "Sophia and Annie" made their farewell and final visit to the town and provided a comic and musical entertainment for 2/-, 1/- or 6d to a large audience.The churches too had their social life. The Wesleyan Young Mens' Christian Association, active in Driffield since 1866, had a programme of discussions, recitations and essay reading.Other social events included fifty local traders attending the Tradesmen's dinner at The Keys and a pigeon shoot that nearly went sadly wrong. Not only were the birds difficult to see against the snow that had been a feature of the intense cold of January, but a by-stander was shot in the heel of his boot when a gun a gamekeeper was replacing in a case, went off. Mr Jackson advertised his East Riding Almanack and prepared his annual display of Valentines from 1d each in his shop.

There were 1199 inhabited houses and a further 92 empty houses in Driffield in 1871. Many of these had been built in the previous forty years and to a great extent they were zoned and streamed along social lines. Leaving the farms aside, the top of the social scale was

the detatched villa with a spacious garden that might even be classed as grounds.The majority were on the outskirts of the town and were the homes of solicitors (Southorpe Lodge, Rose Villa), corn millers (Beechwood and White Hall) and the more prosperous merchants (Mill Hill) but others were to be found in a more central position. "Mr Whiting's newly erected houses" occupied only one side of Downe St. leaving space and privacy for Chestnut Villa on the other side of the road, the home of George Hodgson, another solicitor. A similar pattern was to be found on Brook St. where terrace development was confined to one side leaving a solicitor and a retired barrister to occupy more substantial houses on the other side of the street.Semi-detatched villas, usually nearer the town centre, were nearly as private, cost less to build and "gave the casual passer-by an impression of being grander than they actually were".[1] Leo Villas, built by the artist and engraver Alexander Lydon in the 1860's on land released by the railway company in Beverley Road, is of this type.

Elsewhere in Driffield the terrace was the normal development characterised by the straightness of the row and the sameness of the houses. Winding roads, trees and gardens were expensive and at odds with the interests of the developer who was often, in Driffield, a shopkeeper who had bought a plot of land on which to erect a terrace of cottages for rent. William Turner's four cottages on Mill St. and Morris' Buildings in Paradise Close were built or acquired as a secondary source of income by a wine and spirit merchant and a butcher. Terraces, and by implication the people who lived in them, were "respectable" but subject to fine gradations, "the lower the class, the plainer and more frankly terraced the house". [2] The most respectable terraces were marked by bay windows, porches, decorative string courses and a narrow garden between front door and street.The terrace in this elaborate form had hardly reached Driffield by 1871, though it was to become a common pattern for the rest of the century. The houses in Church St. are an example of the better Driffield terrace of 1871 but more typical are the nine houses

11

built in 1842 as Lora Cottages in Eastgate and occupied in 1871 by the respectable working class; journeymen shoemakers, tailors, ironmoulders, and cabinet-makers. At the other extreme the lowest class of terrace had no embellishments. Whilst still "respectable" in 1871 many labourers lived in "straight rows of brick boxes cut into by rectangular door and window spaces". [3]

Below the terraces in terms of social differentiation were the courts, the yards and the buildings. These were marginal areas in terms of respectability and likely to be much more densely populated .Gibson's Buildings occupied the site of the former workhouse in Middle Street. Durham born Edward Gibson, the developer of Gibson St., had acquired the unwanted building to house his iron and brass foundry. In addition it housed a school and was home to forty-five people. The courts of North End were clearly looked down upon by many in Driffield who perceived them as a home of crime and possible social disturbance. It is interesting to see the way in which the court type of development has reappeared in Driffield in recent years, although they are rarely called yards by modern developers.

Lodgings in Victorian times carried a different implication from today. Lodging houses were overcrowded and unsanitary. They offered a bed often of dirty straw in a communal room and board "usually consisting of some common cooking facilities". [4] They attracted the migrant workers, the new arrivals in town, the Wold Ranger seeking a winter roof, the out of work and the underworld of criminals and semi-criminals. Mary Tucker, the tramp who summoned the North End lodging housekeeper Martha Berriman for assault, was not untypical. The occupants were often on the lowest rung of the social ladder but one. Some lodging houses doubled as brothels like John and Martha Berriman's two cottages at North End, occupied by the seven Berrimans, all but one adults, and fifteen lodgers from Ireland, Scotland and six English counties. A description of this particular lodging house exists from the first decade of the Twentieth Century. "A small common lodging house where tramps or down-and-outs could stay the night and cook anything that would cook over a huge fireplace at one end of the long kitchen, which was ..... knocked into one. The upstairs had been opened up in the same way.[5] Robert Plummer's very small cottage also in North End had, in addition to his own family, ten lodgers including a family of five from Lincolnshire, a married couple from Hull and three labourers. Such groups did not qualify to be "respectable" and lived at only one step removed from the workhouse.

It is perhaps necessary to distinguish between the lodging houses and houses where lodgers were taken in. Then as now, widows and couples whose children had left home, took in lodgers. Married men offered lodgings to single men who worked alongside them in the cake and corn mills.Apprentices lodged with the master's family. Thus of the twenty-five houses in Brook St., seven had lodgers all of whom were in steady jobs. There is no need to deny such people the status of respectability and Brook St. was not untypical of many working class streets in Driffield in 1871.

The population of Driffield had doubled since 1831. The vast majority of people attracted into the town came from the surrounding East Riding so that by 1871 only a quarter of the household heads and their partners had been born in Driffield. (See Appendix 2) The other Yorkshire Ridings, Lincolnshire and Norfolk were the next most common source of immigration but thirty-one other counties were represented, as well as Scotland, Ireland and Wales. Such an inflow of people from different areas must have widened hoizons in Driffield but it was a more cosmopolitan society than might perhaps be supposed. At the height of British imperialism it is not surprising to find people born in the West Indies and India. The Ezard family of watchmakers in Middle St. had evidently been emigrants to Australia and had returned to Driffield, as had Sophia Botterill, the wife of a solicitor. Three families included members born in America, whilst George Leighton, the grandson of an agricultural labourer in Moot Hill, had been born in Paris. Given that

Germany was only unified in January 1871 it is perhaps a little surprising that no fewer than five people (or the enumerator?) gave, in April 1871, "Germany" as their birthplace. In addition to an Austro-Hungarian Count, a Swiss governess , a French maid and a German visitor, the most intriguing residents of Driffield were two Swedish students, Carl Bjoilingson (31) and John Biolin (23) who lodged in Middle St. at the home of John Hildon, a tailor.

It was also a young society. Almost 80% of the population was under 45 (see Appendix 3), which perhaps says something about life expectancy but also underlines the expanding nature of the town as the young and the mobile moved in. At the other extreme , Mary Piercey of Westgate, aged 93 and Thomas Randall aged 88 claimed to be the oldest female and male inhabitants. A word of caution needs to be said over ages and years of birth. Memories fade and there were no birth certificates before 1835. An interesting example is the well known Driffield archaeologist, J.R.Mortimer, who wrote in "A Victorian Boyhood in the Wolds", "I was born on June 15th 1825" and yet gave his age in the 1871 census as 44, which would mean a birth date of June 1826.Thomas Randall was a retired mariner who, fifty years before, had captained the steam packets "Progress", "Hope" and "Speedy" on the route between Driffield and Hull. He lived in a cottage just above River Head, looked after by his housekeeper. Perhaps an old sea dog's last girl in his last port.

REFERENCES:
1.Best : Mid-Victorian Britain 1851-1875:
 Fontana page 36
2 ibid p.37
3 ibid p.37
4 ibid p.45
5 Reffold : Pie for Breakfast:Hutton Press p11

CHAPTER TWO

FEBRUARY

Events in France continued to dominate the
foreign news, but it was not long before local people
were responding to a disaster nearer home. In the early
hours of the 10th February a number of ships were trapped
in Bridlington bay by a S.S.E. gale blowing directly into
the bay."The Great Gale" driving the ships on shore as
they dragged their anchors, wrecked thirty ships and took
seventy lives in the immediate vicinity, despite the
heroism of the two lifeboat crews. One of these, the
"Harbinger" successfully reached five ships but was
capsized alongside a sixth, the brig "Delta",with the
loss of six of the lifeboat crew. The news was received
with particular poignancy in Driffield because the
"Harbinger" had been the gift of a Driffield resident.
Count Gustave Batthyany had been born in Vienna in 1829
into a family of Hungarian aristocrats who were to play a
leading role in the disturbed politics of the Austro-
Hungarian Empire, indeed Count Louis Batthyany, the
Minister President after the Hungarian rising of 1848,
had been executed. Count Gustave became a naturalised
Briton and by 1866 was living in Bridlington where he
learned that the local fishermen felt that the official
R.N.L.I. lifeboat "Robert Whitworth" was too heavy and
difficult to launch from an open beach. Batthyany paid
for a new boat to be built to the fishermen's
specifications. [1] By 1871 the Count had moved to Grove
Cottage in Driffield and was no doubt as shocked by the
disaster as was the rest of the community. There was a
good local response to the appeal fund including an
Invitation Farmers' and Tradesmen's Ball ·in aid of the
widows and children of the lifeboat crew. About a month
later there was a letter from "G.B" (Batthyany ?) to the
Driffield Observer advocating that a harbour of refuge

should be created at Bridlington by building a breakwater on the Smithwick Sand across the exposed face of the bay. It was suggested that convict labour could be used.

However the main preoccupation in Driffield in January and February 1871 was with education and the new Education Act. The provision in Driffield was a varied one in 1871. The more affluent families employed governesses. There were seven in the town, including Fernandé Pietra, a 19 year old Swiss employed by the younger Jarratt to look after his six children. James Jennings, like Jarratt, a solicitor, employed a private tutor. Those who could not afford a governess had a choice of seven private schools. The most important was run by James Firth in "commodius premises erected expressly for educational purposes" [2] on the corner of Shady Lane and Church Street. Firth had thirty-five boarders aged between 10 and 16 drawn from a wide area of the East Riding, together with roughly the same number of day pupils, presumably from Driffield. He employed a 17 year old teacher and "visiting masters" to supplement his teaching.

Mr Auty, who ran an Academy in New Rd., moved in 1871 to the "schoolroom recently occupied by Mr Collins at Gibson's Terrace". The schoolroom, 10 yds x 6 yds x 5 yds high was "one of the most commodius, airy and suitable for the purpose in the town". Mr Collins, who ran a Commercial school, moved into the old workhouse, now known as Gibson's Buildings. He offered 120 places at 6d and 9d a week according to the age of his pupils. It is difficult to believe that the move was beneficial for him as he shared the building with a noisy iron and brass foundry and overcrowded tenements. Perhaps the fact that Gibson owned Moot Hill, Gibson St. and the workhouse had something to do with the move. The Ross sisters Ladies' Seminary in Bourne House in Doctors Lane, Miss Layburne's school in New Rd., the Misses Reastons' school in Exchange St. and the Bell sisters school in Downe St. catered for the private education of girls. At least two of these schools had boarders.

It is difficult to know what proportion of children attended private schools. Later in the year it was estimated at 1/7th but this would seem to have been no more than an informed guess. It would mean roughly 175 children.The majority of children going to school would attend the National Schools at Cross Hill run by the Anglicans and providing an education within the framework of Church of England beliefs.   Mr Greenlaw and Miss Nicholson were in charge of the schools which claimed spaces for 161 boys, 90 girls and 90 infants, with an average attendance of 260.There was also a Mission school for girls at North End. This may have been the same Ragged school that was opened "in the worst part of the town" in the 1860's. It was run as an Anglican school and Sunday school by Miss Holtby and had capacity for 60. It remained as a school until comparatively recently.

There were several Dame schools providing a form of elementary education. Most were in ordinary cottages but at least one was organised by the Primitive Methodists in their chapel in Mill Street. It was estimated that no more than 100 children attended these schools. The provision was very basic as can be deduced from the tactful comment of one of the leaders of the reform group in Driffield. "I have no intention to say a harsh word or make any statement which would for a moment hurt the feelings or injure the circumstances of any persons who have the conducting of these schools."Finally the Poor Law Guardians employed John Everitt at £40 p.a. and Martha Tankersley at £20 p.a.to run the school for workhouse children. Both were praised for their work by Mr Pope, the Inspector of Union schools on his February visit. [3]   Theirs was a floating population but they had some 36 scholars in April.

It was ascertained that there were 1170 children aged 5-13 in the town and that some 950 school places were needed. Even if the contemporary estimate of 1/7th in "the higher schools" is accepted, it is difficult to avoid the conclusion that at the most generous estimation, fewer than 600 of the town's children were attending any form of school in 1871. Since the collapse of the nonconformist British and Foreign Bible Society school in 1847, the provision was overwhelmingly Anglican in nature. This of course was the point. The 1870 Education Act aimed to provide enough school places for all children. Where the voluntary societies, of whatever denomination (but in Driffield's case that meant the C.of E.) were meeting that need, they could be left to continue to provide the area's schools but elsewhere there was now the legal provision to elect a School Board that could levy a rate, build schools employ teachers and, the crucial point, provide an education that was undenominational. In a town with as strong a dissenting tradition as Driffield, this was bound to be an attractive possibility.

The topic dominated. The Driffield Times described it as "all absorbing". "Popular feeling on the subject has attained a rather high temperature and numerous placards and appeals, pro and con, have been published for some days past." For some the Act opened the way for reforms that would provide opportunities that would go beyond providing a basic education. The Observer published a letter from William Porter of Downe Terrace who wrote, "I take it for granted that the first thing aimed at by the new Act is to bring under instruction 1000's of children who are receiving no education at all" but went on to claim that much of the education normally reserved for those attending private schools could be provided in language teaching by the School Board sharing a teacher of German, French and Latin with another town. The agitation reached a "grand climacteric" in a public meeting in the Corn Exchange, chaired by one of the managers of the National Schools, the solicitor George Hodgson, who opened proceedings by drawing attention to the managers' project to enlarge the existing church schools "to furnish ample provision for all educational requirements in Driffield". It was too late, the battle lines were already drawn.

The nonconformists were led by Thomas Whitaker, a Baptist, a sub-post master on New Rd. and himself an ex-National schoolmaster. They put forward a formal resolution "that it is expedient that a School Board be formed for the parish of Great Driffield under the Elementary Education Act of 1870". This was countered by an Anglican amendment proposing a committee to confer

18

with the National School managers about enlarging the existing schools. It is worth examining the arguments that Robert Tonge, another solicitor, and his seconder, William Jarratt , advanced for they were to form the basis of the opposition throughout the fight. They fall under two broad headings. Firstly the church schools were run in a very liberal way and despite being financed and run by Anglicans "exercised the utmost religious liberty". No one therefore had anything to fear if they expanded to provide the education for all Driffield children. The second line of argument went beyond religious interests. The government it was asserted, had "ordered that schools would be of a palacious character and might cost £5000". Local ratepayers would carry the burden. The way was clearly being pointed to compulsory education and it was "better (and cheaper!) for parents to act voluntarily".

When the resolution was voted on, the amendment received "a score of hands", the original motion "a forest of hands". At a separate church function a local minister had to face complaints that it had been "a parsons' meeting" though from the reports the solicitors seemed to dominate. Perhaps this serves to underline the genuine public concern in the issue.

The next step had to be a poll of the ratepayers to confirm the desire for a Board, but a second public meeting was called early in February, almost certainly by the dissenters, to rally support for the proposal. "The meeting opened with the social barometer indicating fever heat." The nonconformists had made sure one of their party was in the chair and rejected a move to have Hodgson. Strong speeches by Whitaker and three nonconformist ministers attempted to quell anxieties about the Board, in particular compulsory education was within the discretion of a local board, the fees of poor parents could be remitted and the costs would be "little more than spent on the National Schools".

The actual poll was something of an anti-climax. "It was the surprise of most to find such apparent apathy on the part of the public. Ratepayers came up languidly and the afternoon proceedings were of a very tame character." Out of about 1250 ratepayers, only 392 voted but "there was a large number of working men present who have taken a great interest in obtaining a school board". [4] They saw their cause victorious by 305 votes to 87 and Driffield thus became the second area in the Riding after Hull, to opt for a School Board. The Church party had lost the first round but could still retrieve the situation if they could control the election of the new Board.

There was certainly no apathy. There were 14 nominations. Two were farmers who, given the common attitude of farmers to education in the 19th Century, may be presumed to have been motivated by a desire to protect ratepayers. They stood down before the election, perhaps persuaded by the Church party whose main candidates were Jarrett and Manuel Kirkby (40) a man of independent means who lived with his aunt on Middle Street. The third Anglican candidate was Hodgson whose electoral address showed a marked lack of enthusiasm and who was described as making very little effort. As a party they were organised enough to have a committee and to carry out an "active canvass". The nominations revealed the potential weakness of the dissenters, for each of the nonconformist sects·put forward their man. No doubt the obvious folly of dividing their forces was responsible for the withdrawal of all but Whitaker, a Baptist who was endorsed by the more powerful Primitive Methodists, George Wrangham(50) a Wesleyan and retired merchant living in Westgate House and George Brown, a 63 year old currier and a member of the reformed Wesleyan Chapel on Bridge Street. Like Hodgson, he was said to have made "very little effort" to win election.

Two other candidates were William Bradshaw (39) a gardener and seedsman of Southorpe Terrace and Thomas Marshall (44) a local bank manager. They described themselves as "non-sectarian Working Man's candidates" and were said to have "worked hard for them". Marshall had chaired the dissenters' public meeting which would suggest he was sympathetic to their views. James Jennings (42) was "the last to take any step in the matter but no

20

ELECTION OF SCHOOL BOARD.

PARISH OF GREAT DRIFFIELD.

NOTICE IS HEREBY GIVEN THAT

1. The First Election of a School Board for this Parish will take place on the Sixth day of Ma c ., 18/1.

2. The number of persons to be elected as Members of the School Board is Five.

3. Any two Ratepayers may nominate any one person of full age, but no more, as a Candidate by sending to, or delivering at, my Office in Exchange Street, Great-Driffield a nomination paper.

The nomination paper must be dated and subscribed by the two Ratepayers, and must contain the Christian names, Surnames, places of abode, and descriptions of the Subscribers and of the Candidate nominated.

No nomination paper will be received after 4 o'clock in the afternoon of the Twenty-Third day of February Instant.

4. Public notice will be given of the List of Candidates on or before the Twenty-Fifth day of February Instant.

Any Candidate may be withdrawn by delivering at my said Office, not later than 4 o'clock in the afternoon of the Twenty-Seventh day of February Instant, a notice of withdrawal signed by the Candidate and addressed to the Returning Officer.

5. Notice of the boundaries of the polling districts and of the number and situation of the polling places will be published on or before the Second day of March next.

Each voter must vote in the polling district in which the property in respect of which he is rated is situated, and if it is situate in more than one polling district, in any one of such polling districts.

6. The poll will be open from One p.m. until Eight p.m.

7. Every Ratepayer of the parish is entitled to vote in the election.

8. The voting will be by an official voting paper, which shall be in the following form, or in a form similar:—

OFFICIAL VOTING PAPER

Christian Name, Surname, Description, and Place of Abode of each Candidate.	No. of Votes (if any) given to any Candidate must be entered opposite his name.
A.	
B.	
C.	
ETC.	

Name of Voter _____

Street, Lane, or Place in which Property, for which the Voter appears to be rated is situate.

Voting Papers will be supplied at the polling places.

9. In this Parish each voter has Five votes, all of which he may give to one Candidate, or he may distribute all or some of them among the Candidates as he thinks fit.

Dated this Fourteenth day of February, 1871.

Signed

HENRY BOTTERILL,
Returning Officer.

sooner had he done so than he became one of the most popular of the candidates and if he had come out earlier he would have topped the poll". [5] His was the most thoughtful and constructive of the manifestos and he was the most prominent in public affairs. An attorney, he was the coroner, the clerk to the Magistrates, to the Tax Commissioners, to the Navigation, to the Burial Board and was influential in a host of local societies.

The Observer was prepared to endorse Whitaker and Jarratt as candidates. "The Primitive Methodists have selected (Whitaker) .....and there can be no doubt their choice is a good one. There is no man in Driffield better fitted for the post, from the extensive knowledge he has of the educational statistics of the town." Jarratt's contribution to the National Schools was also recognised, "there is no man in the parish more worthy of the thanks of his townsmen". Quite correctly the editor predicted that "of the others we will say one or two will not come to the poll".

The campaign was hard fought, even dirty. A squib, "a most dastardly production (was) anonymously sent out to gratify an old grudge against one of the candidates". The voting system also leant itself to party manipulation. Each ratepayer had five votes that could be cast in order of preference or as a block in favour of one or more candidates. There is clear evidence that the organisers tried to use this to party advantage. On polling day "vehicles of nearly all descriptions bearing impressive mottoes and labelled with unmistakeable instructions relative to the candidate for whom you must vote, were driving about in all directions". "Invalid women, who had not been out for many weeks, were impressed and carried into the booths, some in arm chairs." "The bustling and excitement and the rattling and dashing of cabs, carriages and other vehicles were characteristic of a borough council on a small scale."

It was estimated that 935 ratepayers voted, a 75% turnout. The results for the final nine candidates were :-

```
WRANGHAM (Wesleyan)............914
JENNINGS (Peoples Candidate)...877
WHITAKER (Primitive Methodist).771
JARRATT  (Church of England)...634
BRADSHAW (Working Mans Cand.)..584
-----------------------------------------------
KIRKBY   (Church of England)...573
MARSHALL (Working Mans Cand.)..262
HODGSON  (Independent).........74
BROWN    (Independent).........23
```

The voting threw up some interesting points. Jennings was the most popular candidate with 381 individual voters prepared to support him as compared with 370 for Wrangham. Significantly 275 ratepayers voted for Kirkby as compared with 218 for the successful Bradshaw. As the Driffield Times noted, "Mr Bradshaw's success is therefore entirely owing to the concentrated support he received". Analysis shows that 52 people allocated all their votes to Bradshaw whilst only 28 did so for Kirkby. If the Church party had been able to organise their votes better they might have secured the election of Kirkby over Bradshaw, thus giving them a much more powerful voice on the Board. As it was the war was effectively lost. Jarratt was left in isolation to try to preserve the Anglican position, but as will be seen, there was no question of surrender.

At the first meeting of the Board in the Corn Exchange, Jennings was elected Chairman and Wrangham Vice-chairman. The appointment of William Wigmore to be clerk at £20 p.a. perhaps owes something to Jennings' influence, since he was his managing clerk as well as being his deputy coroner, but it has to be said that Wigmore was clearly the best qualified of the three candidates.

REFERENCES
1 Fawcett : The Bridlington Life-boats p17
2 Hull and East Counties Herald :28-1-69
3 H.C.R.O. :PUD 9/2/71
4 Hull Advertiser : Feb. 1871
5 ibid : March
6 ibid : March

CHAPTER THREE

MARCH

Few people in Driffield had the vote in 1871. In 1867 an Act of Parliament gave the vote to working class men in the boroughs but for the county constituencies the right to vote was much more restricted. 1867 extended the vote only to £12 householders, by definition middle class, which meant that in the 1868 General Election only 294 men voted in Driffield plus a small number of plumpers who had pledged all their votes to one candidate prior to the poll. These did not include the future M.P. for the area, Luke White. The plumpers were not recorded in a way which allows the number in Driffield itself to be identified but there were only 362 for the whole district. Since there was no ballot the votes were recorded openly.[1] In the County as a whole the two Conservative candidates, Christopher Sykes and Harrison-Broadley were returned with a comfortable majority but in Driffield, the Liberal, Haworth-Booth secured the most votes, 143, against 142 for Sykes and 63 for Harrison-Broadley. At a time when there was a strong correlation between Liberals-Dissent and Conservatives-Anglican, this is not surprising but what is interesting is the way that the voters responded to the form of proportional representation in practice. Each voter had two votes to cast but many Liberals chose to use only one vote. By 1871 eighteen £12 claims were sustained and five new freeholders added to the electoral roll. This in itself confirms the rate at which Driffield was expanding but it meant that in 1871 only some 500 men at the most had a vote out of a population of 5269.

Nor was there a local council to vote for. Instead a variety of overlapping bodies had responsibility for local affairs. The oldest of these bodies was the Vestry meeting, in essence a parish meeting open to all. Historically concerned with choosing church officers such as sextons and parish clerks, it was also a vehicle for discussing wider parish issues, particularly as the parish was the financial unit for raising money. Sometimes the meetings were the occasion for sectarian battles. Thus proposals in 1861 and 1862 to repair the church by levying a church rate of 1¼d in the £1 were objected to by dissenters who demanded and got a poll of ratepayers to defeat the suggestion.Yet the Vestry did perform necessary tasks as three meetings in the Spring of 1871 show. Having purchased the 7 acre burial ground for £1400 in 1863 it was the Vestry which appointed a Burial Board to administer it.It was the Vestry meeting which approved the recommendation to spend £200 in 1871 to maintain the lighting in the town and on the upkeep of the ancient fire engine "so far as its very limited capabilities permitted", fixing a rate for the purpose of 3 d in the £1.   It was the March meeting that appointed parish constables, overseers of the poor and highway surveyors, although each of these was also responsible to a different authority. The meetings were very sparsely attended, typically by the shop-keepers and craftsmen who took their turn in office. 15-20 was the normal attendance though any threat of an increase in the rates was likely to lead to a demand for a public meeting and a poll of ratepayers.

A more powerful body was the Board of Guardians, based upon the catchment area of the market town and supervising poor relief in the area. In the 1871 election, George Hodgson and John Robinson, a local farmer, were elected by the local ratepayers as Guardians for Driffield and the tanner, William Foster, for Little Driffield. The Board of Guardians was the main claimant upon the rates. In 1871 Driffield had a rateable value of £20,350 and Little Driffield £975. The Poor Law assessments came to £1248 and £56 in 1871. The Poor Law Guardians exercised wide authority over public health issues in the town, since Driffield had not set up a local Board of Health as it could have done under the 1848 Act. The Guardians had the authority to check public nuisances as when they ordered the highway surveyors of Little Driffield to provide a cess-pool in Horsefair Lane and entered into a protracted battle throughout March with John Postgate, who had moved to Birmingham, to force him to provide some sort of drains for the tenants of his three cottages in Little Driffield [2] When the poll was held to decide if a School Board was desirable, it was the clerk to the Poor Law Board who was responsible for the arrangements and acted as Returning Officer.

The confusing state of local government was a source of irritation at the time. A leader in the Driffield Times (borrowed from the Daily Telegraph) pointed out that "the existing plan of collecting the rates or local taxes is at once confused and wasteful. The Poor rate, the Highway rate, the Burial Board, the Lighting and Watching rate...... are collected some by one authority and some by another, but all by officials over whom the ratepayers have not sufficient control and who work under cover of obscurity." The School Board would soon establish a further body making demands upon the rates.

Realistically the ultimate authority in the town lay with the J.P.'s through the Petty Sessions, normally held every other week in the town, and the Quarter Sessions at Beverley. They had influence that went far beyond their administrative and supervisory functions or the dispensing of justice. "If the small tradespeople and shop-keepers were to be eligible to act as......members of local boards and Guardians, at least let the Bench of Justices remain the preserve of the gentry." [3]

They were capable of behaving in an idiosyncratic manner as two of the cases that came before them illustrate. At 9.00 one evening, John Sawdon (13), Thomas Green (13) and John Whitaker (14) stole a pork pie and eight black puddings from a shop in Middle Street. They put the goods under their coats and walked away but were spotted and arrested. The two magistrates sentenced John Sawdon to fourteen days in the House of

Correction at Beverley and then five years at Castle Howard reformatory. Whitaker and Green each went to Beverley for a month and in addition, Green received a whipping. The Bench "was only sorry that in the case of Whitaker that the statutary whipping could not be given as he was just two days beyond the age allowed for whipping". Sawdon's father was later summoned to court to pay a 1/- a week maintenance out of his wages of 8/- a week to keep his son at Castle Howard. It is probable that Sawdon "a most disobedient and wicked lad to his mother" according to the police evidence, had been in trouble before but one can not help contrasting his treatment with that given by the same two magistrates to Charles Taylor (17) who was employed as a groom at a house behind the grocery warehouse of Henry Angas. He was found guilty of stealing various kinds of nuts and two bladders of lard from the warehouse and hiding them in the stables, but was let off with a warning, his "parents being so respectable". No doubt Sawdon, Green and Whitaker failed the respectability test.

Any discussion of how Driffield was administered and controlled in 1871 would be incomplete without reference to the police. Supt. Harper lived in the town police station and lock-up built in Eastgate in 1843 but the dominant personality would seem to be Sgt. Thomas Wood (39) who clearly had a formidable reputation in the town and was obviously a figure of respect, if not of fear. The force was completed by P.C. Charles Hoggard (23) who was said by the local paper "to lose no opportunity of making a raid on some of those dens of iniquity at the North End of the town". What their working relationship was to the parish constables appointed by the Vestry is not clear but between them they policed a town that was often lively and where disturbance was never far below the surface.

The Justices were not beyond criticism, but apart from on one occasion to be dealt with later, it was mild. The local paper complained about the increased issue of licences to pedlars by which "any lazy lout is furnished now with a diploma in the form of a few ha'porths of tape or buttons to enter into peoples' houses and plunder when convenience admits". The same source also criticised the reduction in the cost of dog licences. "You can't approach a house scarcely in the town, but out leaps a snarling cur or a savage brute from which you are glad to make a retreat. On the Sunday a.m. too, scores of dogs are taken out on the roads and in the fields for the purpose many of them, for the pursuit of game."

Perhaps it was the fine weather and the thought of Spring evenings that brought people out of doors. Mr Taylor had several first class velocipedes and Mr Rayner had a 36" front wheel bicycle for sale. Robson, in the Market Place, advertised his Spring fabrics of fancy Scotch angola trouserings and fancy vestings and was offering "a real good sound and well shrunk suit for 60/-". There was still a number of indoor attractions arranged in March. The Buck opened its new billiard room and filled it soon afterwards with a challenge match between the champion and ex-champion of England, W.Cook and J. Roberts. Signor Bosco drew a large audience to the Assembly Rooms for an evening of magic given by him with bare arms, without sleeves, without coat pockets, without covered tables and without any assistance, but the most popular event was a talk on Biblical archaeology given by a member of the Palestine Exploration Society in a crowded Corn Exchange.

An indication that winter was passing came from the master bricklayers in the town, in essence the builders, who fixed the 'summer' hours of their labourers as 6 a.m. to 5 p.m. on Saturdays. The 'winter' hours from November to March had been 7 a.m. to 5 p.m..The builders who combined in this way were Clark, Dandy, Leason, Dry and Berry.On the Wolds the Spring wheat was being sown. The wet November the previous year and the long winter had done severe damage to the clover and much of the crop had been ploughed in. Gardeners looked at seed potatoes on sale at Raylor's at 6d a stone and considered varieties such as early Racehorse, Lapstone, Pattison's Victoria, Ash Tops, Myatt's Prolific and Prince Regent. Near the end of the financial year, the Guardians asked for tenders to

28

supply blue linen check, shawls and straw bonnets for female paupers and grey calico shirting, cotton cord and strong rustic hats for the men. Local hairdressers tendered for the contract to cut the hair and shave the paupers.

On a wider stage the local papers considered, with approval, the Secretary for War's proposal to abolish the practice of buying army commissions but it was the events in France that horrified and fascinated the leader writers. After the defeat by Prussia, the outbreak of revolution in Paris led to the creation of a radical, socialist commune that opposed the official government. "The crumbling away of all authority, the state of disintegration into which France is sinking are but the natural consequences of the first revolution .... the revolutionary torrent has again been let loose and there is no hand powerful to stem or direct it." A demonstration in Hyde Park by the International Democratic Association, a group of English Republican sympathisers, drew such little support that in a mood of self-congratulation and conscious superiority over the way the French conducted their affairs, the Driffield Times could write, "if French republicanism were so harmless as the English republicanism that aired itself on Sunday evening, France would be a happy country".

REFERENCES
1 Beverley library : 1868 Poll Book
2 H.C.R.O. : P.U.D. 9/3/71
3 Redich and Hirst : History of Local Government in England : p177

CHAPTER FOUR

APRIL

At the approach of Easter the beautiful weather and the prospect of a holiday led people to concentrate on outdoor activities. The landlord of the Falcon, Mr Partington, organised the Easter Sports in his field "near the railway station on Wansford Road". Spread over two days, there were prizes for events ranging from pony races, a pedestrian handicap, a high jump won by "a gentleman amateur" and the main event, a 150 yard handicap sprint for a £10 prize that attracted " some of the best runners in Yorkshire". For those who disapproved of the thought of competing for money at Easter, the Wesleyans organised a social tea for 350 and the Congregationalists organised their own Sunday School sports with children scrambling for nuts and oranges. It all helped to create a holiday atmosphere of bustle and activity, particularly as the Easter Fairs drew large numbers of additional people to the town for the traditional sale of horned cattle and sheep.

One would have expected the census to have dominated local discussion in April but it seems to have passed smoothly and to have aroused little comment. The Superintendent Registrar was the solicitor, William Jarratt, the son of the School Board candidate. His clerk, John Brigham was appointed assistant registrar. They recruited a team of eight enumerators, mostly clerical workers such as Solomon Parker, John Brown and George Thirsk, the grocer who was also a solicitor's clerk and the Registrar of Births, Deaths and Marriages. Paid 21/- each plus 2/6d per 100 entries over 400, they had the schedules distributed to households by March 27th ready for the census day of Sunday, April 2nd. Allocated to the areas in which they lived, they had the completed forms to the Registrar by April 7th.

The census confirmed, not unexpectedly, that Driffield was a town that had an economy based firmly on agriculture, but one that had become an important local market and commercial centre with a minor administrative role as the centre of a Poor Law Union and a County Court district. The canal head and the railway at the junction of the line over the Wolds to Malton with the Hull-Scarborough line, gave it local importance as a centre of communications. The way in which it was expanding by attracting people into the town, has already been noted, as has the age structure of the town, where nearly four out of every five people were under 45. It all added up to a vigorous expanding economy in which only seventeen males claimed to be unemployed. This was 1.1% of the male population between the ages of 15 and 80, though such a figure disguises the casual nature of many labourers' jobs.

There was a manufacturing element to the economy which, for the most part, served and underpinned the town's agricultural base. After the census had been taken, Charles Dawson took over the blacksmith's in New Rd. after the death of the owner and developed it to make and repair agricultural machines. Both he and the well established George Foley, who employed eleven men at his works on Middle St., advertised three and two horse reapers, weighing and winnowing machines, straw and turnip cutters and oil cake crushers. Foley had been a manufacturer since at least 1850. If these two actually made the implements, much of the work of the thirty-nine men employed as blacksmiths in the town must have been in repairing the machines.

The most important manufacturing business was the Driffield and East Riding Pure Linseed Cake Company. They had impressive buildings on a prime site in the town alongside the railway so that goods could be loaded directly from the works and horse-drawn railway waggons shunted into the body of the factory along their own branch siding. Situated opposite the coal staithes and within a 100 yards of the canal head, it was in an ideal position. The works had been extended in 1870-71 by the addition of a south wing and connecting buildings.It now

THE DRIFFIELD & EAST RIDING PURE LINSEED CAKE COMPANY LIMITED.

stood four storeys high, crowned with a clock tower complete with a chime of five bells. The company had been formed in 1861 by local farmers and stock breeders to meet a specific need. The key word in the company's title was 'pure'. Linseed had long been imported into Hull from Russia. It was then made into oil-cake, an artificial feed for sheep and cattle. The problem was that it was a trade open to fraud. The Chairman of the Driffield company was William Jarratt (senior), the bank manager, who wrote a pamphlet in 1870 outlining the problem. Despite the snappy title, 'The Character and Condition of the Linseed Cake Trade considered in relation to the Manufacturer and Consumer with suggestions for putting the Business on a more Satisfactory Basis', Jarratt's book did give a lucid outline of the problems. There was widespread adulteration of the seed by Russian merchants and British manufacturers who added weed seeds, sand and other "earthy matter". Many producers made little attempt to produce high quality cake but sold feed to the farmers that was so adulterated as to be almost worthless. The trade was so corrupt that there were stories of Hull ships leaving port to rendezvous with incoming ships in order to sell them the waste material removed from previous cargoes of linseed so that it could be added to the next shipment coming in.

Local farmers responded by forming the Driffield and East Riding Pure Linseed Cake Company in 1861 to manufacture a cake in which they could have confidence. The process involved screening the linseed to remove the smaller weed seeds and other impurities. The seed was then crushed between rollers and processed into animal cake. At £13 a ton the feed was expensive, but it clearly had the confidence of the farmers who had a large say in running the company. Although he wasn't the first Chairman, it was Jarratt who guided the company through the expansion of the premises and the diversification into cotton cake, and was able to announce a record half-year to the shareholders in 1871. It was almost certainly Driffield's largest employer.

FAT BEASTS AND SHEEP.

MATTHEWS'
CORN FEEDING CAKE,

Either used alone, or given with pure or genuine Linseed Cake,
hastens the feeding properties.

Food mixed for Feeding purposes is proved to be the cheapest, the
quickest, and the best mode of Feeding Beasts and Sheep. The flesh
and fat of animals are sweeter when fed on Matthews' Corn Cake.

MANUFACTURED BY

F. C. MATTHEWS, SON, AND Co.,
AGRICULTURAL CHEMISTS, DRIFFIELD.

PRESENT PRICE—£9 10s. AT THEIR WORKS.

MATTHEWS'
SPECIALLY PREPARED MANURES FOR ALL CROPS.

ESTABLISHED 23 YEARS.
Manure Works, Driffield, 1871.

In March 1871, the Driffield Observer had a leader which stated "Driffield is . particularly identified with the origin and extension of the application of artificial manures, which owe their success in a great measure through the individual effort of Francis Cook Matthews. The agricultural world is much indebted to his foresight, energy and perseverence." When Matthews established his company in 1847 he'd found a great deal of prejudice amongst local farmers at the idea of using bones dissolved in sulphuric acid as a fertiliser and he had to work hard to "induce a few of the more intelligent farmers to try an experiment with them", but by 1871 Matthews Son and Co. were manufacturing artificial manures and animal feeds in two mills in the town.

Matthews lived in Easterfield House on the corner of New Road. His son, also called Francis Matthews, was an agricultural chemist, who lived almost opposite. Their main factory was opposite the modern car-park in Eastgate and the remains of the works can still be seen, in much altered form, behind the manager's house that is still intact.

Matthews' 'Little Mill' has survived in a much better state , also on Eastgate, but behind the park. They produced a wide range of chemical fertilisers which they contrasted favourably with Peruvian guano at £12 a ton. They advertised nitro-phosphate for turnips, rape and mangolds at £6 10s a ton, ammonia-phosphate for wheat, oats, barley and grass at £10 10s a ton, a potato manure, dissolved bone manure and crushed bones at £8.00 a ton. On the feed side they produced corn feed cake and oil cake for ewes and store beasts.

In Little Driffield, William Foster had a manure works and tannery employing thirteen people and as was to be expected in an area such as Driffield, corn milling was important. The two wind-mills were no longer operative. The North End wind-mill had lost its five sails in a storm in 1860 and Henry Angas removed the rest when he moved into Mill Field Hill. The Wansford Rd. wind-mill was taken down about the same time. [1] Leaving aside Bell Mills, which was outside the town boundary, there were four corn mills driven by a combination of water wheels and steam power. The most substantial miller was William Witty of White Hall, who farmed 253 acres, had a corn warehouse at Riverhead and operated Albion Mills. Dawson of Beechwood was the owner of Poundsworth Mill but had suffered a disasterous bankruptcy in 1870 and the mill may not have been operational for a time in 1871. George Harrison was a corn factor who had a warehouse and corn milling business at Riverhead and Henry Marshall was the miller at King's Mill.

One manufacturer in the town whose business was not based on agriculture was William Taylor, who manufactured sewing machines in a large wooden shed on Eastgate, on land belonging to Matthews. His machines were successful but expensive at four guineas upwards, which perhaps accounts for the formation of a sewing machine club in which people were invited to form a section of twenty members each paying a subscription of 2/6d a fortnight until the section had raised £7 to pay for a machine. The twenty then drew lots to see who got the first machine, but continued to pay a subscription until all twenty had "the absolute necessity" of a machine. Taylor employed six women in 1871 as sewing machinists, one of the few alternatives to domestic service in Driffield.

Benjamin Fawcett also employed girls, some as young as 13 and 14, as colourers in his printing works in East Lodge. Fawcett's was a highly successful business that produced high quality printing. His method of producing part-works has been written about elsewhere [2] but by 1871 the major force in the firm was perhaps Alexander Frank Lydon, who produced a prolific amount of work. An Irishman by birth and a Royal Academician, he stayed with Fawcett until 1883 when he moved to London to work independently. One work, 'The Country Seats of the Noblemen and Gentlemen of Great Britain and Ireland', had 240 coloured plates each requiring separate blocks for different colours. They were said to have all been done by Lydon. He still found time, perhaps influenced by his seven children, to produce a little poem 'Fairy Mary's Dream' which he illustrated with seven coloured plates and small wood engravings and which Jackson sold locally for 6/-. The presence of Fawcett's works and the three newspapers in the town was reflected in the large number of printers in Driffield, thirty-four in all.

There were two important coach-builders. William Roberts worked from Middle St., whilst Arthur Stott had his works in the original Methodist chapel in Westgate, a building which had also been the Mechanics' Institute in its time. Between them they built phaetons, (light four wheeled open carriages), two wheeled dog-carts, whitechapels used by shopkeepers for local deliveries and gigs (a light two wheeled one horse carriage). A waggonette to carry six to eight people cost £12 from Roberts in 1871. The 74 year old Francis Bradley and his grandson also ran a coach-building firm in Bridge Street.

The family firm of Turner was one of the oldest in the town. They were book-sellers, brewers, sold wines and spirits and ran a brick and tile manufactury next to the cemetery on Nafferton Road. They employed eighteen men to make the dark coloured distinctive bricks that still give a mellow appearance to many of the town's houses. Metalworking was important in the town. There were several whitesmiths but the iron and brass works were more significant. Peter Sibree was a hydraulic and general engineer, a boilermaker and millwright, who had an iron and brass foundry at Riverhead. Gibson's foundry in the old workhouse has already been noted but the most important metalworker in the town was Thomas Pickering, the nephew of a retired ironmonger, Thomas Atkinson, who had largely been responsible for the development of New Road. Pickering certainly had the Albion foundry in 1871 and an ironmonger's shop in the Market Place. His business was expanding for he purchased the moulds and patterns of Samuel Johnson, an ironfounder in Doctors Lane in 1871. Whether Pickering also bought Johnson's crane and crane ladles or the 35 cwt. capacity furnace isn't known. Johnson was leaving the country. Nicholson, writing in 1903, [3] says that Pickering built the

37

Victoria foundry on the site of the first workhouse at Cross Hill in 1854. Nicholson is usually reliable and there would seem to be no reason to doubt him, but it is curious that no contemporary reference to the Victoria foundry has come to light for 1871. Whether there was simply a change of name and the Albion foundry became the Victoria foundry later in the century is not clear. There can be no doubt however that Pickering's business was an important one, employing forty men. Their work can still be seen in the many cast iron pumps that still adorn odd corners of the town.

The factories and workshops were dangerous places in which to work. John Lill, aged 62, a lodger in the shop in Little Driffield, worked in Foster's manure works and tannery. One morning in January he was moving a 100 lb bottle of sulphuric acid in a wheel-barrow along a plank. The barrow slipped and overturned. The bottle broke and the acid poured over his face, neck and chest leaving him severely burnt and blind. There was no inquiry, no mention of compensation and presumably John Lill was unemployable and dependent upon the charity of his landlord, an agricultural labourer. George Cozens worked for the Linseed Cake Company. Perhaps confused by the recent extensions to the premises he walked into one of the monster cisterns for storing the oil and had to be rescued by a colleague from the 15 ' deep tank. Fifteen year old James Kitson lost two fingers, cut off by the blades of a lawnmower that was attached to a machine to revolve the blades as he oiled them. He worked in Alton's engineering shop in Eastgate. John Baker, a cartman, was helping to dismantle and move an engine from a warehouse in Adelphi Street. The bedplate of the machine, a slab of iron weighing 6-7 cwts, was being manhandled onto a truck when it slipped and fell on both of Baker's legs, breaking them in several places.

There was an inquest on William Adam. He was employed by Mr England of Middle St. to feed corn into a thrashing machine. Having stopped for 'allowance' or drinking time at 9.40 and being "perfectly sober" having "no beer but a pint", he returned to the platform of the machine where he slipped on some loose corn and straw. His foot went into the opening of the drum and was drawn in betwen the beaters. It was some minutes before the machine could be halted and his foot remained stuck. Two local doctors amputated the foot whilst Adam was still trapped and he was dispatched home to Gibson St. on a rulley. Scotchburn, the Medical Officer for the Poor Law Union attended him "as it was a legitimate (case) for the parish". Adam died some days later. The inquest noted that "there is a sad want of protection in these steam thrashing machines" but made no recommendations in returning a verdict of accidental death. It should be "a pleasure to the public to know that everything that medical and surgical skill can achieve has been employed for a poor man, to an equal extent as though he were the wealthiest man of the town". The remark was doubtless well intentioned but there is an implicit assumption behind the comment that wealth equated with desert. Such an assumption underlay much Victorian thinking.

William Temple also had an accident with a steam threshing machine. He had a provision shop in Middle St. that he left his wife to run whilst he did odd jobs to supplement their income. In July he was working as a labourer for Ashbridge, an engineer, who was fitting a coal box to the boiler of the machine. The boiler had been taken off its frame and was propped up at an angle on wooden supports. Temple was working partly inside the coal box, turning the rivets as they were hammered through from the outside. Space was cramped and Ashbridge removed some of the props to create more room. He testified that he might have knocked away a prop when swinging his hammer. The boiler slipped, fell on Temple and crushed him. He left eight children. In this case, his fellow tradesmen organised a collection and raised £51 6s for his family. The verdict of the inquest was accidental death.

These were by no means the only industrial accidents in Driffield in 1871. People fell off scaffolding, legs were crushed by mill-weights, hands mutilated by circular saws, but in no case was any responsibility attached to the employer or compensation paid to the workman. Accidents were clearly accepted as one of the risks of the job. There is no record of any trade union activity in Driffield in 1871.

REFERENCES
1. Ross : Contributions towards a History of Driffield: 1898
2. Howorth : Driffield I700-1860. A country town in its setting : p93.
3. Nicholson : The Capital of the Wolds: I903

CHAPTER FIVE

MAY

Towards the end of 1870 Thomas Dawson , the head of the family firm of corn factors and an extensive landowner in the town faced bankruptcy and charges of embezzlement. The charges were dismissed but the firm still had debts of £45,447 and it was no doubt the need to liquidate the company's assets that led to the auction on May 20th 1871 of the prime commercial site in the town, the block of land from the Bell to the Corn Exchange.

The tenant of the Bell was Mrs Kirby. Unfortunately she doesn't appear in the census, presumably being out of town on April 2nd. Her son, Thomas Kirby (30) was a prominent auctioneer in the town and conducted the auction. Lot 1 was the Bell itself, described as a first class family and commercial hotel and posting house. The accommodation consisted of a large bar, a commercial room, six best and other sitting rooms, suitable kitchens, dairy, laundry, cellars etc.. In the large yard behind was a double coach house, three cab and omnibus houses, eight single horse boxes and stabling for up to forty horses. There were hay, straw and other chambers as well as a large piggery. Above the stables was a warehouse leased to a local shopkeeper. The lot had a reserve of £5200 and the bidding reached £4500 from a solicitor, Tonge, probably acting for a client.

Lot 2 was the two shops between the Bell and the corner of Exchange St., together with Dawson's offices round the corner. They again failed to reach the reserve but attracted a bid of £2050 from Pickering, the ironfounder. Lots 3, 4 and 5, various offices, shops and warehouses, including the printing presses of the Driffield Times, failed to attract any bid. When the auction failed to sell any of the individual lots the whole property was auctioned with a reserve of £11,000. Bidding reached £10,000 from Mr Wrangham of Westgate House.

Rivalled in the 18th Century and in the early 19th Century by the Red Lion and the Keys, the Bell was the leading hotel by 1871 and its one time rivals were no more prominent than the Buck, the Black Swan and the Falcon with its "well-aired beds". It had a residential staff of eight and no doubt had additional daily servants. Henry Burks, the ostler, would not have been able to look after the extensive stabling by himself and Mary Stott, the 29 year old cook, would have expected considerable help in the kitchens. A billiard-marker, a 14 year old page, two chamber-maids and two bar-maids completed the staff. There were two commercial travellers among the three guests on Sunday April 2nd, no doubt met off their trains at the station and conveyed with their luggage to the Bell in the hotel's omnibus.

There was no shortage of pubs in Driffield. There were 27 inns and beer houses, one for every 184 of the population, though as a market town they also catered for the many people from the catchment area who used the shops and markets. No less than eight of the pubs were run by women. The inns were valuable commercial properties. The White Horse, part of Turner's estate when he died in 1870, was sold for £660 to Thomas Jefferson, who also owned the Langley Arms. The Rose and Crown at Little Driffield was valued at £750.

The pubs were served by a number of local brewers all operating on a fairly small scale. Mary Holtby's brewery at the bottom of what is now Laundry Lane, was managed by her son, who lived in Bridge Street. Matthew Hewson combined his Springfield Brewery at Riverhead with his other activities as a builder and raff and timber merchant. There was a long established brewery on Middle St. bordering the park, whilst Brewhouse Lane (or Harland's Lane) had one maltkin and at least one and possibly two breweries on it. One of these breweries was operated by the Turner family, who also had one of the two wine and spirit shops in the town.

Drink was not only plentiful but cheap. Ale sold at a 1/- a gallon, a bottle of gin cost 2/- at the Buck, cognac 18/- a gallon and scotch 19/- a gallon at Jessop's wine and spirit shop. Drink had a marked effect on the life of the town. "If there is one evil in this district which stands out more prominently than the rest, that of drunkenness is the one, and from the annals of our Petty Sessions, a daily increasing one." Even a cursory glance at the sources shows the justice of that statement. It is very difficult to convey the extent to which drunkenness was an everyday event in Driffield in 1871. It dominated the Petty Sessions week after week and must have accounted for the vast majority of cases dealt with by the police, indeed the impression is that apart from drink related cases, Driffield was relatively free from crime. The police tried to enforce the licensing laws. Early in May the indefatigable Sgt. Wood was watching the Golden Fleece at 11.00 a.m. on a Sunday morning. He "saw a man with something rather bulky go into the yard. He (Wood) went round to the back window and saw Henry Johnson reading a newspaper. He emerged with a large brown jug and half a gallon of ale." Anne Train, the landlady was fined 10/- with 8/- costs. It was her third offence that year. The Bench could and did threaten to remove the licences of publicans who broke the law, as when they warned the landlord of the Nag's Head for serving George Etherington at 6.30 in the morning. Etherington was already drunk when he arrived at the pub.

People were drunk at work. James Carr was selling fish in the Market Place when he was arrested by Sgt. Wood for being drunk, throwing the fish around and using language not suitable for the crowd of children who had gathered round him. When Matthew Botterill was dismissed in May by one of the brewers, William Howden, he took his coat off and attacked his employer. Normally a mild man, his defence was that he was drunk. Barely a week went by without a waggoner being brought before the Bench for leaving his waggon on the road whilst he resorted to the pub, or, as in the case of a driver named Craggs, being so drunk that he was incapable of driving the horse, so that the cart, the reins and the horse got so "skelled-up" that the horse hanged and died in the traces whilst Craggs staggered helplessly in the road. It is impossible to believe that many of the accidents at work were not exacerbated by drink and it is a fitting irony that when inquests were held they were invariably held in a local hotel.

43

It is possible to trace the activities of families by their regular passage through the courts. Elizabeth and Edward Whitaker lived in Westgate with their five children. He worked in a corn mill. Their relationship is best described as stormy. In the summer he appealed to the court for protection against his wife. She had told him she would cut his throat whilst he was asleep. When drunk she had thrown a poker at him which had stuck in his shoulder. When she appeared in the stand with her face and eye in a bran poultice, the court decided that Whitaker's plea was a pre-emptive move and sent them both away. Early in September she was back in court for being drunk, dressed in Boulton and Park style (of which more later) in male attire. The same month she was drunk in Church St. and "had as usual given police a great deal of trouble to get her in to her own house.....(where she) commenced abusing her children". Her husband appealed to the police to take her into custody. Mrs Whitaker denied the charge of being disorderly and with a friendliness brought on by familiarity, maintained possibly with some justice, "he would bring me here every day of the week would Charlie Hoggard". When the J.P.'s sent her to the House of Correction for seven days she gave "a pleasant smile and said 'Thanks Mr Clare'".

Still in May, Samuel Johnson, "a North End worthy" was arrested by P.C. Hoggard in Westgate. "The defendant was very drunk and pulling his mother about." For knocking her down and otherwise abusing her, he was fined 5/- with 9/- costs. By August he was facing his tenth charge of being drunk and disorderly. Violence and drink were of course common companions. The landlord of the Tiger brought a charge of wilful damage. The defendant "came to my house tipsy and broke the pitchers on the table, the front window and the bar window, in all about twenty panes". The damage was assessed at £5. The defendant was the landlord's son. Landlords (and ladies) clearly had a difficult time controlling Victorian drinkers. John Brown, the landlord of the White Horse, tried to refuse entry to one of Driffield's more notorious characters, John Berriman. "Knowing that he was very bad company" and seeing that he was already drunk, Brown stood at the door to prevent him coming in, but in the resulting fight was stabbed with a hay-fork.

The Bench faced with a steady stream of drunk and disorderly cases seem to have handed out fines between 5/- and 9/- with costs of 8/- or 9/-, perhaps the equivalent of a week's wages for a labourer. Occasionally a more frequent visitor such as John Leak was fined 40/- and 9/- costs for his fifth appearance in a short time, or like Elizabeth Whitaker given a spell in custody. It is possible that the Bench saw her behaviour as more reprehensible in a woman. Faced with the steady stream of cases to report, the Driffield Times often resorted to phrases like "a devout admirer of John Barleycorn", "a quartet of North End worthies" or "all Northenders". A good example is the report of the case of Robert Sedman, the town's bill-poster and "a regular pest. Frequently drunk and insulting people...... he was so uproarious in the street that the defendent's wife had to assert her supremacy and send him to bed about 9.00. Defendent was about to deliver himself of a learned harangue when the Bench put on the extinguisher." Perhaps such reporting is no more than an attempt to lighten the catalogue of repititious cases but it may also be a sub-conscious way, and a patronising way, of distancing the respectable ranks of society from "the North End worthies".

It is clear however that drunkenness was not confined to the labouring classes. On May 6th Joseph Higham, a Kilham surgeon, wrote to the Driffield Times following his conviction for assault. He'd been involved in a pub brawl with Thomas Gardham for attempting to seduce the latter's daughter and had been accused in his turn of thrashing his own wife. It was not the revelations of his private life that worried Higham so much as the accusation by Gardham that he'd been drunk. His protestation in his letter that "any of my friends will testify that I am never guilty of overuse of narcotics of any description and moreover my professional knowledge precludes the possibility of anything of the kind" was undermined later in the month when he was turned out of Dry's shop in the Market Place in the middle of the afternoon for being drunk and ran down the street scattering handfuls of bootlaces taken from the shop.

The above accounts are only a fraction of the cases that appeared before the Driffield courts in 1871. Viewed from a century away they can bring a smile, but they help to explain and justify the various temperance movements that were active in the town. The Band of Hope, the Temperance Society and the Total Abstinence Society held teas in the Corn Exchange, heard lectures on the Government's new licensing proposals, on the liquor trade and on the causes of intemperance, but the audiences were "only limited". In Driffield at least, the movement was essentially a nonconformist one and the Driffield Observer, in reporting a lecture by a visiting Anglican speaker, administered a rebuke to the local Church of England ministers. "As so much apathy is manifested by the ministers of the established church, at least in this part of the country, to lend their help to any movement for the improvement of the working class except those connected with the establishment, Dr Gale deserves the best thanks."

Being the month of May, Driffield Cricket Club began its season, or tried to, as the first game was postponed because of the wet ground. There had been an organised club in Driffield since at least the 1850's playing on a field off Scarborough Road. There is no record of where the matches were played in 1871, but it was not on the present ground. The club was the preserve of the middle class, the time needed to play cricket alone precluding all those who had little leisure. The social standing of the club was seen by the stature of the President, Christopher Sykes and the Vice-presidents, Jennings and Reynard, a J.P. from Sunderlandwick. The eight man committee was made up of people like John Brigham, the secretary of the Building Society, Henry Botterill, the solicitor and Ralph Teal, a china and glass dealer in the town. He may have been the club captain in 1871; certainly he captained the Driffield XI on the 19th May when they played a XXII of the club in a practice game. The names of the 33 players confirm the nature of the club as drawing its members from the professions, the tradesmen and the leisured classes of the town. Francis Matthews took eleven wickets for Teal's side which may mean that he is the only Driffield cricketer to take eleven wickets in an

HORNSEA v DRIFFIELD JUNE 1871

CRICKET MATCH.—DRIFFIELD v. HORNSEA.
—A Match was played at Hornsea on
Monday June 26, and was won easily by
Hornsea on the first innings — the bowling
of Drake proving destructive. Musgrave,
Higginson, Fearne, and Drake batted well
for Hornsea, as did W. A. and R. C. Brown
for Driffield. The following is the score:—

DRIFFIELD.
1st inns.

R Teal b Musgrave	2
W A Brown c Wade b Drake	14
G R Young c Wade b Drake	3
G Hewson b Drake	0
W Dunn b Drake	2
R C Brown not out	20
T Dickinson c Drake b Musgrave	1
F C Matthews b Drake	6
J Crust c Fearne b Drake	0
W Witty b Drake	12
W Fawcett st Scott b Drake	4
Extras	1
Total	**65**

HORNSEA.

Rev A T Mitton c Teal b Dunn	10
J M T Musgrave run out	35
T C B Dixon c Teal b Dunn	0
M Higginson b Dunn	22
J L Fearne c Teal b Hewson	18
G J Drake not out	18
O E L Ringrose lbw b Hewson	0
R J Wade b W A Brown	0
Rev O P Scott b Dunn	10
G Milner c Matthews b Hewson	1
A Brittlebank run out	0
Extras	22
Total	**136**

DRIFFIELD 2ND INNS.—R Teal b Musgrave 8; W A
Brown not out 24; G R Young run out 1; G
Hewson not out 7; R C Brown c Wade b Brittle-
bank 6; extras 6,—total 52.

innings! Wickets in those days were 'sporting' and the scores were low, perhaps not surprising against a side that could deploy 22 fielders. It was reported that the batting and bowling was good, but some improvement might be suggested relative to fielding. Perhaps they got in each other's way. Supper at the Bell no doubt got the season off to a good start.

There were matches arranged against Beverley, Malton, Hull and Hornsea for the first team and several matches for the second team, including Brandesburton and Flamborough. Some appear to have been all-day games played over two innings. The influence of the railways can be seen in the fixture list but the trips to Hornsea and Brandesburton were presumably made cross-country by waggonette or by a lengthy railway journey via Hull. The club did not have a successful season but all went well except that relations were strained with the Brandesburton and Hornsea clubs, who were accused of fielding a team of 'ringers'. Perhaps the fact that Driffield lost heavily in both games had something to do with the complaint that "many of them are picked men. The Driffield club ought to be acquainted with the parties whom they have to meet and not to go blindfold to contest with a set of men picked from the different towns for the occasion."

Everyone in the town had an opportunity to relax over the Whit holiday. Mr Partington arranged a gala in his field on Wansford Road. In part this was for the benefit of the Driffield United Brass Band, which played a leading part in many of the social functions of the town including "performing selections from the newest and most select music" in the market place on Saturday evenings. They put out an appeal for help to purchase new instruments, "their old being in a deplorable condition" and they were sufficiently well regarded in the town for a subscription to be opened to pay the £30 that the new instruments cost. The profits from the Whit Gala were to be donated to the fund.

The band played throughout a day of bicycle races, walking and running races, a high jump competition that was won at 4' 2" and a comic song competition. There was Dancing on the Green during the day and a Grand Ball in a marquee at night. Perhaps some

48

of the ladies wore dresses from Manchester House, Mr Dry's draper's shop, where "newly returned from London", he was offering black silk dresses at 39/-, 44/- and 59/-. Dry was Driffield's McGonagall composing a number of excruciating verses that he used as adverts for his draper's business.

"Just visit Manchester House and view its selection
And there's only one conclusion you'll come to
That a larger or cheaper or better selection
Was never before placed for the public to view

New dresses and jackets the greatest variety
To please you and serve you they are sure to try
And whatever your rank in English society
There is none to surpass or compare with F.Dry's"

Meanwhile the Driffield Times was enjoying a whiff of scandal, reporting with a certain amount of ill-disguised glee, a London High Court case that lasted much of May.Two men, Boulton and Park, were part of a London set who "frequent places where men of loose life and women of light character congregate". The men dressed as women with "painted and powdered faces" and mixed with theatrical women, who dressed and behaved as men. The involvement of the aristocracy in the shape of Lord Clinton added spice to the gingerbread. The papers tut-tutted, gave a full report of the case in which Boulton and Park were acquitted of homosexuality and then congratulated themselves on reporting a case that many had wanted held in camera.

On a more serious level, the papers reported with horror and incredulity, the murder of the Archbishop of Paris and 64 hostages on May 24th by the embattled revolutionaries inside the Commune.

CHAPTER SIX

JUNE

Early in June the 8th Corps of the East Yorkshire Rifle Volunteers mustered on Pinfold Hill, went through their various drills and then formed into line and, headed by the Driffield Brass Band, marched to the home of one of their sergeants to congratulate him on his promotion to Ensign. The Volunteers had been formed in response to a period of anti-French feeling in 1859. The 8th Corps, the Driffield Corps, had an establishment of 60 in 1871. They paid for their own uniforms and in the early days, for their own weapons and ammunition, which inevitably limited their membership to the middle class and in the Government's thinking, there was always an element of guarding against a popular uprising in their establishment. Resplendent in their uniforms of mid-grey with scarlet cuffs and scarlet seams on the trousers, the Driffield Corps had a reputation for size and physique and were at one time nicknamed "the Heavy Brigade". [1] In 1871 they were led by Capt. Edward Lucas, a retired goldsmith, who lived at Bridge House. Lt. Wigmore, the recently promoted Ensign Holtby and Sgt Rawlinson were the leading figures, but like many of the Volunteer Corps they recruited a professional soldier as Drill Sergeant. Sgt Campbell of the 8th Regiment of Foot was appointed in June soon after the Corp's annual training, which brought 271 of the Volunteers from the whole of the Riding to Beverley Westwood for a period of 21 days. The Corps had an armory at Cross Hill on the corner of Beverley Lane and drilled there from 8-9 p.m. three nights a week. The fact that the drilling continued at that hour throughout the winter months implies that they either had a drill hall attached to the armory or access to a building large enough for the 60 men.

The Driffield Anglers was another social activity that was limited to the more affluent. They had 10 miles of fishing locally, but membership was gained by a 10 guineas entrance fee and an annual subscription of a further 10 guineas. Subscribers were allowed six cards a season to distribute to friends each of which allowed a day's fishing. The Anglers employed three keepers, who had cottages on the river. The head watcher, James Leaf, lived at Mulberry Cottage near the old paper mill.

The lighter evenings and the warm weather encouraged people to parade along the favourite walks in Driffield, a pastime made more pleasant by the improving state of the roads. The Justices had a responsibility to review the work of the Highway Surveyors and were critical of many of the roads in the area "as being in very bad condition with deep ruts and loose stones" but in Driffield itself a programme to improve the footpaths had started in 1870. "Once roughly paved, deeply indented side-walks have given place to the half-elastic, hot-pressed asphalted ones." Eastgate, Gibson St, the several lanes, Westgate had all been done with the aid of "a large heated roller". By June of 1871 this programme had been extended to include "the greater way to the cemetery, Moot Hill, the whole length of East Parade and Wansford Rd down to the (railway) gatehouse, the station to Beverley Lane junction and then to the National Schools." The last section was a favourite promenade because it was well lit. Nor was it just the footpaths that improved, for in October the surveyors were using "a patent street machine" to sweep the roads. The new machine, "a large brush the size of a land roller made of cane or whalebone, is made to move in a transverse direction to the road". It was said to cope well with "the very dirty and sloppy state of the roads" and replace the "twelve sturdy scavengers" previously used to sweep them.

For those who wished to make their own entertainment at home, Jackson offered new and second hand pianofortes and harmoniums for sale, but at prices ranging from 25 gns. to 150 gns., they were expensive enough to warrent him offering hire purchase terms over three years. Jackson and the other local booksellers had a good stock of books ranging in price from 5/- for 'The Boy's Treasury of Sports and Pastimes' to 15/- for 'Our Lakes, Mountains and Waterfalls' which was illustrated by photographs. Dickens 'The Mysteries of Edward Drood' was on sale at 7/6d.

For many people social life centred around the churches in the town and demanded total commitment by the whole family. Chapel teas, the Young Mens' Christian Association, Temperance lectures, choir practices, Bible classes and prayer meetings in the week and services on Sunday could fill the leisure time. Particularly in the nonconformist groups, which tended to be dominated by laymen, many men were helped to grow in self-assurance and a sense of self-esteem by being helped in the Sunday school as a boy, helping as a monitor and then taking a class before progressing to become a lay-preacher. The Sunday schools attracted impressive numbers. Whitaker, who was in a position to know, made it his business to establish the numbers attending the different schools as part of his School Board campaign. He quoted the Church of England as having 70 scholars, the main Methodist Church (the Wesleyans) as 190, the Methodist Free Church 50, the Primitive Methodists 300, the Congregationalists 220 and the Baptists 50. If one excludes babies, this would imply about half of the town's children attending Sunday schools. [2]

The Baptists had moved from the chapel in Chapel Lane, which was occupied by the Sykes Lodge of Freemasons, to a new chapel on Middle Street. The Primitive Methodists were in Mill St. but would move in 1873 to an impressive building in George St. which would reflect their following in the town. The sad shell of this building still exists as a warehouse, but without its dominating towers and its front pediment it is difficult to sense its former size and importance. The Primitive Methodists were an undoubted force on the Wolds and Driffield had been a circuit town since 1837. Woodcock described their following as belonging "to the middle and respectable classes".[3] The local preachers were working men, who spoke in the language of their congregation. "Thousands who had sunk to the level of dull monotony unbroken from year to year....found in ....soul stirring preaching, services, fervent prayer meetings, lively class meetings and hearty singing,... a life freedom and joy to which they had been strangers. Methodist chapels have long been the centres around which the religious life of these villages has resolved. They feel at home there as they do not at the parish church." [4] The Wesleyans perhaps had a more middle class flavour about them in Driffield, but they were an active and thriving body. Something of this comes across in their 'Home Mission' in 1871, an attempt to establish a place of worship in the upper room of a barn in one of "the dark places of the earth ", North End, among what the Times called "the full grown City Arabs of the district". The different Methodist sects were more a matter of organisation and personalities than of doctrine. One of these splits had resulted in the United Methodist Free Church establishing itself in Bridge St. in a chapel that has recently been restored in a way which reflects the standing of these groups in the community. The Congregationalists were in Exchange Street.

How far did all this activity reflect genuine religious feeling, whatever that means, in Driffield society in 1871 ? The churches could certainly exert a considerable influence when they thought the occasion needed it, as the School Board elections show. The fact that Boak, the local photographer, found it worth his while to offer photos of local clergy for sale in his shop, must say something about the influence of the churches. However convention plays its part. To be seen attending church or chapel was a mark of respectability and of standing in society. Perfectly properly, the church was a centre for social activity, for developing and sustaining friendships, for meeting the opposite sex as well as for worship. The distinction between religious devotion and conformity is impossible to quantify.

Once the School Board was elected and a clerk

appointed, the members held weekly meetings from the end of April. The first problem they had to tackle was the question of for how many children they were supposed to be providing. No one knew with any certainty. The question was politically important because the smaller the number the easier it was to argue that the existing buildings were adequate and the less need to spend money on a non-denominational board school.

Both sides staked out their positions. Jarratt was in favour of enlarging the National Schools at a relatively small cost to the ratepayers in preference to spending some £4000 on new buildings. This, together with the 938 school places he estimated to be already in the town, would provide all that was needed and would retain the control of education by the church authorities. Whitaker, after proposing that the managers of the National Schools should be invited to transfer the existing buildings to the Board, argued that the number of existing places was 850 and that a 1000 were needed.

The Board decided on two measures. They would write to the Education Department to discover how much extra school accommodation was needed. Ever helpful, the Department replied that the Board from a local standpoint was in a better position to decide the need for places than they were, but the Department "reserved to. themselves the power of finally determining the amount of extra school accommodation required". Secondly, after a proposal by Jarratt to give three men a guinea each to carry out a house to house survey, the Board commissioned the secretary of the Poor Law Union, at a cost of £33-0s-6d to carry out a survey of 3-5 year olds and 5-13 year olds. Before he had an opportunity to report they decided on a third measure. They would write to the census authorities and pay 14/- per 1000 entries to have the number of children extracted from the recent census.

The meeting of June 14th was a lively one. The clerk to the Poor Law Union gave it as his opinion that 50/1000 of the population were aged 3-5 and 80/1000 aged 5-13 and that would give a total of 1170, of which he estimated 1/7th attended "the higher schools". There was a need therefore to provide 953 places. (When the census return was available in July it showed 1226 children aged 3-13). Jarratt questioned the figures, pointing out that the National Schools proposed extensions for 100 places were not included, that the number of places in the Mission school was under-estimated and he revealed that he was going, at his own expense, to provide a room 75'x 120' in Harland Lane to supplement the existing accommodation by a further 208 places. Under the circumstances there was no need to consider a new school.

Whitaker led the counter-attack. There were already sufficient Church of England places available and the church party already had more than their fair share of access to Parliamentary grants. He reminded Jarratt that they had been refused an increased grant in 1862 because in the view of the Education Department, "the dissenters of Driffield outnumbered by far the party seeking to obtain a grant of public money for church school purposes". He accused the National School managers of trying "to frustrate the intention of an overwhelming majority of the inhabitants of the town, expressed at several public meetings and at the poll booths, to establish schools of an unsectarian character". What was more the Anglican control over education would be perpetuated because they would prevent members of the other sects becoming pupil-teachers and then school-teachers

Despite the attempt of Wrangham to calm proceedings down, the meeting became animated with Jarratt accusing Whitaker of taking "a sectarian view of the affair and he reviewed at some length what voluntarism had done in teaching the youth of Driffield". The voluntary provision would be extended by his new school room. This was too much for the rest of the Board who gave Jarratt's school room, situated in a warehouse above a brewery, short shrift. "A public house at one end of the lane, a common brewery at the other end, a maltkin opposite, a manure depot on the left and a ginger beer manufactury on the right, piggeries and stables on one side and stables and manure heaps on the other, I can not conceive that any person in Driffield (except the one whose unprofitable property the old brewery happened to be) could ever have dreamt to establish a school in such a place."

This, the most significant of the Board's meetings to date, ended with a proposal from Bradshaw to build new schools on the eastern side of the town as soon as a possible site could be found, since the town was divided by Middle St. into two halves and the existing schools were on the west side. The proposal was carried and the meeting ended.

Not everyone saw these moves as progress. It is worth quoting in full a letter from George Whiting, the grocer who had developed Downe St., written at the end of the year when events had moved on and the divisions within the School Board had deepened even further. The letter is interesting not least for the contemporary recognition that many of the developments of the town over the last thirty years were due to the energy and enterprise of people moving into the town. Whiting's was probably a minority view, but there was, to play on words, more than a grain of truth in his criticisms of the Corn Exchange, whilst his thinly veiled attack on Whitaker, "our dissenting wind-bag" was probably more than a personal view when it is realised that Whitaker was the target of the squib at the time of the School Board poll.

The letter to the Driffield Observer is headed:

A Fast Town

The progress and public spirit of our fast little town, cannot but excite the surprise and pity of our more staid and sober minded neighbours. They must be convinced that we are an enterprising people. They don't know that we owe most of our unnatural growth to a few leading spirits imported from large towns, with a large notion of taxation and parochial expenditure, and small means to sustain them. We are an ambitious people. We built a magnificent corn exchange, so vast that when two or three corn factors took possession of it, or rather a nook and corner of it, on the market day, they were so impressed by its vastness and their smallness, and the impossibility of hearing each other for the echoes, that they took up their desks and walked. The fact is , as the gentleman said who opened it, we built for future generations, and we have the satisfaction of knowing that, though the building be too large for the present, it will stand for centuries to come, a monument to the enterprise and folly of an ambitious people.

We are a far seeing people. We build for future generations. We had a workhouse nearly new and too large by half for the requirements of the Union. Our wealthy neighbours, with a population of one hundred thousand, found it necessary to erect an immense bastille, and forthwith we proceeded to imitate them. We bought half a farmstead and erected a palace-like building, capacious enough to contain the entire population of our little town. Under ordinary circumstances and with the present increase in the rate of population, it may be fully occupied a thousand years hence. We have just added an immense plot of burial ground to the old parish graveyard. We were blessed with a good peaceful old vicar who never asked awkward questions, but in his large souled charity, consigned all alike, good, bad and indifferent, to a hopeful future. But our leading spirits with commendable forethought seeing that we were not provided with sepulture ground enough to last til the morning of the resurrection, agitated a cemetery. We have now two temple-like structures surpassing anything you can see from John O'Groats to Lands End, with a sufficient number of acres to last through all time.

We had first class public schools, infant and ragged schools, all provided and sustained by private benevolence or voluntrayism, supplemented of course by government grants; if more school accommodation were wanted to meet the requirements of the Elementary Education Act, private benevolence offered to supply it. We are an independent people and we spurned the offer with righteous indignation; at least our School Board did. And if they had done nothing else all the time they have been elected (and what else they have done it is difficult to say), they would have been justified in the demands they have made upon the overseers for the first instalments of costs of their ornamental, if not useful existence. We ought to be proud of our School Board. What little town the size of ours can boast of a School Board and such a Board! so considerate so deliberate. Twelve months have been expended in discussing what ought to be done, and what might not be done. The amount of elecution, gesticulation, and splenetification expended by our dissenting wind-bag, has been something stupendous. His has been a noble task, a task worthy of his great powers of blatancy, to pour on the devoted and venerable head of the churchman and educational champion of the past, in one continued stream, the lava of dissenting wrath until he was consumed from the Board. We must live by faith. We have the promise of the Board of good things to come in the shadows of the future "of a good time coming"-- that when the preliminary discussions necessary to a mutual understanding between churchmen and dissenters are complete, and the wind-bag is exhausted, which may happen in the course of this century, that then they will purchase an estate on the east side of the town, which side of the town is said by one of the Board who resides there to be the most deficient in education, and there erect a college for the accommodation of the rural arabs that may and will hereafter be born. The shooting on the grounds to be reserved to the Board alone.

It is supposed that when this project is accomplished the taxes will cover the rents, and swallow them up, and the whole town will be pauperised. And it needn't surprise any of our neighbours if some fine morning they should meet a procession of the entire population of our independent and enterprising town, moving solemnly and with becoming dignity towards the unoccupied bastille, headed by the leading spirits of the town.

G.W.

Whiting is the articulate and authentic voice of conservatism in Driffield in 1871.

REFERENCES

1 Wilson and Collinson : East Yorkshire Voluntary
  Infantry 1859-1908.
2 Driffield Observer : December 3rd 1870
3 Woodcock :Piety among the Peasantry: being Sketches
  of Primitive Methodism on the Yorkshire Wolds : 1889
  (p88)
4 Ibid p262

CHAPTER SEVEN

JULY

Driffield, as a flourishing market, attracted the commercial and professional services that were necessary to serve the businesses of the town and the surrounding area. It had three banks, the York Union Bank where Robert Galt, the Scottish manager lived above the premises, Jarratt's East Riding Bank and the Burlington and Driffield Bank managed by T.G. Marshall. The East Riding Bank had been designed by Cuthbert Broderick, the architect of the National schools, and like its rivals, occupied impressive stone fronted buildings. All three were open six days a week from 10 a.m.-3p.m. (5p.m. on market day and 1 p.m. on Saturdays). The Driffield Savings Bank on Exchange St. had local worthies like Reynard, Wrangham and Angas as President and Directors. It had 1777 depositors in 1871, mainly from humble backgrounds. 258 of the savers had between £5 and £10 in the bank and the fact that £1271-12s-3d was deposited with the bank at the end of November, pointed to most of their customers being involved in the November hirings. William Taylor was employed as manager at £70 a year and had an assistant at £30. The Post Office Savings Bank provided an alternative for those labourers who were unlikely to approach the commercial banks.

The Driffield and East Riding Benefit Building Society had been formed in 1865 to "enable many an artisan and labourer to become the owner of his own dwelling". It offered £50 shares that could be bought at 2/- a fortnight and paid a dividend of 8% to shareholders in 1869. In 1870 it had a healthy balance of £51,555 and had attracted deposits of £7418 on which it paid 3½% interest. At a time when it was rare for the working class not to rent houses, it would be revealing to know how many did use the society to own their own houses.

Then as now, many of the solicitors were concentrated in Exchange Street. There were nine in the town working in four, possibly five, practices. The most prestigious was probably that of James Jennings, where William Wigmore was the junior and managing clerk, but the most interesting is the practice of George Hodgson, if only because his general clerk was Luke White. Aged 26 in 1871, White had been born in Deighton and educated at Foss Bridge School in York. He had married the daughter of a York currier in 1869 and was living in a terrace on Scarborough Road. A Primitive Methodist, he worked his way up from office boy to qualified solicitor and became a partner in the practice when Hodgson retired in 1874. Entering politics he was elected to the first East Riding County Council in 1889, becoming an alderman, county coroner and political agent for the Liberals. He was elected M.P. for Buckrose in 1900 and knighted in 1906. By then he was living in White House on Beverley Rd., had an expensive life-style in London to sustain and, at a time when M.P.s were not paid, faced two expensive general elections in quick succession in 1910. It was about that time that he ran into difficulties, but he survived until 1919 when he was arrested for embezzlement of £19,000 of his clients' money. Too ill to face trial, he died in the workhouse infirmary.

Various people in the town acted as insurance agents, invariably on a part-time basis. They included George Jackson, who added yet another string to his bow by representing the West of England Company. John Morris was the only accountant in town, but there were two auctioneers, John Brigham, who combined the work with that of Registrar of Births , Deaths and Marriages, and Thomas Kirby. There is no architect listed in the census but John Frank Shepherdson, the cabinet maker who employed twelve men in what was acknowledged to be the leading woodworkers in the town, appears in a directory of 1872 as a licensed valuer and building surveyor and in the Driffield Express of 1872 as an architect. It is probable that he worked at both the design stage and in the construction with the local tradesmen who were so often the property developers in Driffield and with the seven local builders who built the terraces and villas. By the late 1870's he had several architectural commissions for public buildings in the area.

As was to be expected, the larger more prestigious shops were to be found in the town centre, clustered around Market Place and Middle St., whilst all over the town were to be found the small general and corner shops that were often left to the wives to run whilst the husband had other work. Thus Mrs Verity ran a fish shop in Brook St., selling fish which her husband, a waterman on the canal, no doubt brought back from the Hull fish market. The distribution of shops in the town is shown on the sketch maps in the appendix. It hasn't always been possible to show on the sketch maps that shop-owners often combined different retail lines, so that for example grocer and draper was a common combination. Appendix 4 shows the number of men employed in different areas but it too needs to be treated with caution. The distinction between craftsmen making things and shop-keepers retailing them is a blurred one. The eleven saddlers in the town appear in the 'trade and craft' section but they could with equal justification appear under 'retail' as workers in the shops of Lundy and Pinkney, the two saddlers in town. The boot and shoe makers are another obvious example of people who combined making items and helping to sell them in the same business.

In an age when everything in the grocer's shop was weighed and packed on the premises and when people tended to shop every day for food, it is not surprising to find large numbers of people employed in the grocery trade. The 19 errand boys in the town, the youngest 10 year old William Brown from Moot Hill, is one pointer, but a further indication is the way in which many of the larger shops had assistants and apprentices living above and behind the shop. Ross, the draper on Middle St., employed five men and two boys, six of whom lived with him on the premises. It meant that they were readily available to man the shop, often until 10.00 at night. The Driffield Times announced with approval that many shop-keepers were closing early on Saturday nights at 9.00 p.m.. This "privilege" would allow shop-assistants to make suitable preparations for the Sabbath.

Labourers and the other poorly paid, might use "the clothing club established in 1853, for the working class (in) cheap Manchester House", but Dry's establishment would still be too expensive for many who were more likely to look to Edmond's in North End, who wanted "second hand clothing of every description" to sell. Some too would use the Co-operative stores in Doctors Lane. This had been established only in 1868 and had a sticky start, actually losing £40 in the trading year 1869-70. There were hints of mismanagement, if not of misappropriation, but a change of manager allowed the society to pay a dividend of 9d in £1 to its 80 members and 5d in £1 to non-members. For many of the poorest people the 'divi' was the only form of saving that was open to them. The Co-op was also less likely to sell adulterated food than elsewhere. The 107 tenants, who cultivated the 27 acres of allotments on the west side of the town, had access to cheap food, but many would rely on the Thursday market with its supplies of fruit, vegetables, butter and eggs.

Market days produced an inflow of people from a very wide area. The streets were crowded, not just with people and stalls, but from the carriers' carts parked in Cross Hill and outside the pubs, which were used as the boarding points. These, plus the waggons and carriages that had brought people into town, created a bustling scene. Accidents, such as the one when a man was kicked in the face by one of the horses outside the Keys, were not uncommon. The degree of influx can be gauged from the diagram, which shows that 103 carriers attended Driffield market every Thursday, bringing people as well as goods. In addition a horse-drawn omnibus came from Beeford and Skipsea and one from Helperthorpe returning at 5.30, which must have meant a difficult journey in the winter months. Other people of course, would come in by train, perhaps catching the 'government' train to take advantage of the cheap fares. The influence of the railways on the carriers can be

CARRIERS ATTENDING DRIFFIELD MARKET 1871

① THIXENDALE
① POCKLINGTON
① GOODMANHAM
① WARTER
③ FRIDAYTHORPE
① FIMBER
③ HUGGATE
① KIRBY G'DALE
② W & E LUTTONS
② HELPERTHORPE
③ WEAVERTHORPE
② MIDDLETON
② N. DALTON
② LUND
② FRANTON
② WETWANG
① SLEDMERE
② GARTON
① KILNWICK
① KILHWICK
① SOUTHBURN
② TIBTHORPE
① KIRKBURN
③ BESWICK
② LOCKINGTON
① HUTTON
② CRANSWICK
① AIKE
① FRODINGHAM
① WANSFORD
④ LANGTOFT
① FOXHOLES
① WOLD NEWTON
③ THWING
② BURTON FLEMING
③ RUDSTON
⑦ KILHAM
④ NAFFERTON
② KELK
③ GEMBLING
① FOSTON
③ HARPHAM
④ RUDSTON
③ BURTON AGNES
① THORNHOLME
① HAISTHORPE
① BRIDLINGTON
① BRANDESBURTON
③ BEEFORD
① SIGGLESTHORNE
① BEWHOLME
① ATWICK
④ SKIPSEA
① FLAMBOROUGH

64

seen from the diagram which shows that villages on a train route sent far fewer carriers to Driffield than villages away from a railway line. Speed was the main advantage. Malton was an hour away, Bridlington 25 minutes and Beverley 37 minutes by the stopping trains.

The railway was one of the largest employers in the town. It was extremely labour intensive with a gate-keeper, and in most cases a cottage, at every road crossing, with nine porters at Driffield station and 10 clerks employed locally. In all 35 people earned their living on the railway. The Driffield-Malton line struggled financially, showing a loss on workings of £1469 and a total debt of over £52,000 in 1870. Nor was the railway company universally popular. In August, the town Sunday Schools planned a children's outing to Bridlington. They contacted the North Eastern Railway to put on a special train but were horrified to find that the fares quoted were 5½d for children and 11d for adults, as compared with 4d and 8d in the previous year. There were complaints about the monopoly that the railway held and a leader in the Driffield Observer pointed to the difficulties that parents with several children would face. The railway company remained adamant. Nevertheless the trip went ahead with a contingent from each Sunday School marching, complete with banners, from the market place to the station, preceeded by the town band. Whitaker was the commander-in-chief of the 1000 strong force. Despite the fact that the train was late, the party arrived safely in Bridlington, marched behind the band to the Quay and spent the day on the beach before returning at 8.00. The Observer noted that "Mrs Knagg's donkeys were in great requisition and enjoyed the day much less than their riders did". Rather pointedly, it ended with the comment that the railway company had made £30.

The railway company had reason to be grateful for a more modern means of communication when the engine of the 8.00 a.m. Malton train came off the turn-table behind the signal box at Bell Mills Lane, blocking the line. It needed telegrams to Hull and Malton to warn of the blockage before the line was cleared. The telegraph

RAILWAY TIME TABLES.

From Scarborough to Hull.

	Week Days.							Sun.	
	1 2 g	1&2	1 2 g	1&2	1 2 g	1	1 2 g	1 2 g	
SCARBORO' Dep	6 15	7 40	1125	4 40	7 5	a		4 45	
Seamer	6 24	7 47	1133	4 47	7 12	...		4 52	
Cayton	6 32	...	1138	...	7 18	...		4 58	
Gristhorpe	6 37	...	1143	...	7 23	...		5 2	
Filey	6 44	8 3	1150	5 5	7 29	...		5 10	
Hunmanby	6 52	...	1258	...	7 37	...		5 18	
Specton	7 2	...	12 8	...	7 47	...		5 28	
Bempton	7 11	...	1218	...	7 56	...		5 38	
Marton	7 16	8 26	1223	5 27	a	...		5 43	
BRIDLINGTON	7 30	8 40	1240	5 40	8 15	...		5 57	
Carnaby	7 36	...	c	...	8 21	...		6 2	
Burton Agnes	7 44	a	1348	5 50	8 29	...		6 9	
Lowthorpe	7 49	...	1256	5 54	8 35	...		6 15	
Nafferton	7 55	a	1 2	...	8 40	...		6 20	
DRIFFIELD	8 3	9 8	1 10	6 7	8 49	9 40		6 28	
Cranswick	8 13	...	1 17	6 14	8 58	b		6 38	
Lockington	8 23	...	1 25	...	9 0	b		6 46	
Arram	8 28	...	1 30	...	9 11	b		6 51	
BEVERLEY	8 40	9 29	1 42	6 37	9 25	10 7		7 5	
Cottingham	8 53	9 38	1 53	6 47	9 35	1016		7 15	
HULL Arrive	9 10	9 50	2 10	7 5	9 50	1030		7 30	

(a) Stops to set down from Stations beyond Filey, and to take up for Beverley and Stations beyond.

(b) Stops when required.

(c) Stops on Thursdays to take up Driffield Market passengers.

From Hull to Scarborough.

	Week Days.							Sun.	
	1 2 g	1&2	1 2 g	1&2	1 2 g	1	1 2 g	1 2 g	
HULL	6 30	10 10	12 35	4 55	6 0	8 40	7 0	
Cottingham	6 40	10 21	12 44	...	6 11	8 49	7 10	
BEVERLEY	6 50	10 35	12 56	5 11	6 25	8 59	7 24	
Arram	7 4	10 44	1 5	...	6 34	b	7 30	
Lockington	7 9	10 49	1 11	...	6 39	b	7 40	
Cranswick	7 19	10 59	1 20	...	6 49	b	7 46	
DRIFFIELD	7 30	11 10	1 33	5 32	7 0	9 25	8 0	
Nafferton	7 36	11 16	1 39	a	7 6	...	8 5	
Lowthorpe	7 42	11 22	1 46	...	7 13	...	8 10	
Burton Agnes	7 47	11 27	1 50	...	7 17	...	8 15	
Carnaby	7 56	11 36	1 58	...	7 26	...	8 21	
BRIDLINGT'N	8 15	1	8 15	6 2	7 40	...	8 35	
Marton	8 23	1 7	2 23	6 7	7 45	...	8 42	
Bempton	8 37	...	2 32	...	7 53	...	8 46	
Specton	8 44	...	2 37	...	8 0	...	8 51	
Hunmanby	8 44	...	2 47	...	8 10	...	9 5	
Filey	8 52	1 30	2 57	6 29	8 18	...	9 13	
Gristhorpe	8 59	...	3 4	...	8 25	...	9 20	
Cayton	9 4	...	3 10	...	8 30	...	9 27	
Seamer	9 14	1 43	3 18	...	8 40	...	9 33	
SCARBORO'	9 25	1 55	3 30	6 50	8 55	...	9 45	

(a) Stops to set down from Stations beyond Beverley, and to take up for beyond Filey.

(b) Stops when required.

From Driffield to Malton.

	Week Days.				
	1 2 g	1 2 g	1 2 g		
LEAVE	a.m.	p.m.	p.m.		
Driffield	8 45	1 40	6 31	...	...
Garton	8 55	1 49	6 41	...	...
Wetwang	9 7	1 57	6 47	...	...
Fimber	9 14	2 3	6 54	...	...
Burdale	9 22	2 10	7 2	...	...
Wharram	9 28	2 14	7 8	...	...
N. Grimston	9 35	2 22	7 15	...	...
Settrington	9 50	2 27	7 19	...	...
Malton Arrive	10 0	2 40	7 30	...	...

From Malton to Driffield.

	Week Days.				
	1 2 g	1 2 g	1 2 g		
LEAVE	a.m.	a.m.	p.m.		
Malton	7 0	11 50	4 39	...	...
Settrington	7 10	12 1	4 51	...	...
N. Grimston	7 16	12 8	4 55	...	...
Wharram	7 21	12 13	4 45	...	...
Burdale	7 27	12 19	4 47	...	...
Fimber	7 35	12 27	4 57	...	...
Wetwang	7 41	12 33	5 3	...	...
Garton	7 51	12 45	5 15	...	...
Driffield Arrive	8 0	12 55	5 25	...	...

66

had only been installed in 1870, with three lines leaving the railway at Mr Robinson's house on Beverley Rd. and going to the Post Office by Beverley Lane. The railways provided an essential part in the work of the Post Office, the mail arriving by the 7.30 a.m. and 5.32 p.m. trains, ready for the two postal deliveries of the day at 8.20 a.m. and 6.30 p.m.. Letters were delivered on 365 days of the year, including Christmas Day, although there was only one delivery on Sunday. One intriguing aspect of the Post Office's work is that houses in Driffield were not numbered in 1871 (though they were by 1879). Presumably in the days when letter writing was, in some respects more limited, the letter carriers had no difficulty in finding the addressees in what was still a small community.

Throughout July the Driffield Times was enthusiastically reporting a case that held the whole country in thrall. It had all the necessary ingredients of Victorian melodrama. Edward Stronghurst, the heir to the £40,000 a year Titchborne fortune, presumed drowned at sea in 1857, supposedly emerged in 1867 from the Australian bush to claim his fortune. Recognised by his mother, his claim was challenged after his death and became the focus of a court drama that ran and ran until March 1872, with fashionable society ladies sitting beside the judge on the bench as he heard the case. The Driffield Times contribution to this soap opera was to print a free engraving 7½" x 6" with the July 8th issue of the paper, showing the two main lawyers, the claimant, Titchborne House, the escape from the ship- wreck and life in the Australian bush. Jackson, the editor, clearly expected it to boost sales, leading up to the event for several weeks in advance and warning readers to make sure of their copy in good time. If it did boost sales, it no doubt helped to create the right atmosphere for the staff's annual outing later in July. Paid for by Jackson, they went to Filey by train, lunched at Jackson's restaurant at Filey, a further Jackson interest, took carriages to Filey Brigg, had dinner at Foord's Hotel and a boat trip in the bay, before returning to Driffield.

Jackson was also responsible for bringing "the unfathomable mysteries" of Maskelyne and Cooke, the Royal Illusionists, to Driffield at the beginning of July. Their act was a mixture of spiritualism and magic, "spirit rapping, table talking" mixed with "the gorilla mystery and the elevation in mid-air of a beautiful female without any visible means of support". At 2/-, 1/- and 6d they were thought to be good value but unfortunately they clashed with Sanger's Circus, like Maskelyne and Cooke, regular entertainers in the town. The circus procession through the streets of "the monster equestrian establishment (and) the ponderous and gorgeous carriages with their richly attired occupants caused a good deal of excitement.", but the very wet weather meant the afternoon's performance was poorly attended.

However Driffield was first and foremost an agricultural community and no attraction in July could rival the Show. The Driffield and East Riding Agricultural Society had not thrived in the period before 1871. There had been no show held in 1869 in deference to the Yorkshire Show which was in Beverley that year and in 1870 the Beverley Agricultural Association proposed a merger with the Driffield Society to hold a joint show which would rotate around the towns of the two Unions. A delegation from Beverley had attended the 1870 annual general meeting to press their case and the Driffield decision to go ahead and hold a separate show had not been unopposed in Driffield. That show had not been particularly successful and there was "a deal of dissatisfaction amongst the tradesmen in the town". The 1871 A.G.M. was therefore crucial to the Society's future. A balance of £1-15s-0d on the 1870 Show and a turn out of twenty did not augur well for what the Driffield Times called "the resuscitated society". The dissatisfaction came to a head over the position of Jonathan Turner as Honorary Secretary. In a move which hinted at the tensions of the last few years, the meeting wished to elect the secretary but Turner insisted that it was the role of the committee and he had to be reminded by Jennings that last year's A.G.M.

had confirmed the right of the full membership to choose. Matthews, the fertiliser manufacturer, proposed Turner, but Jennings was more guarded. "He could hardly agree with Mr Matthews that a better man than Mr Turner could not have been found. He had no personal objection to Turner but he must say that unless there was an alteration in the management of the society it would not be attended with the success that it had been." There had been a species of jobbing and he would prefer to appoint a paid secretary over whom there would be more control. Turner denied "jobbery" i.e. using the post to his own and his friends' advantage and declared that he now expected to be paid. "This announcement seemed to take several members by surprise." They may have been further surprised when Turner declared the proposed salary of £20 to be too small and complained that a paid secretary "would have no perquisites". Jennings' warning that if the jobbery of last year was repeated, the effect on the society would be serious, would seem to have been very necessary. The date of the Show was fixed for Friday, July 28th. A lot clearly depended on the success of the 17th Show.

Economically the Show was very important to the town. There were special trains from Hull, Scarborough and Malton and "the highways converging on the town presented a very animated experience". The eating houses in the town prepared to feed the "teeming thousands from a widely extended area". Hardwick's Eating House claimed to be able to accommodate one thousand for breakfast, dinner and other refreshments. The Bookless Rooms, strategically placed near the railway station, no doubt did equally good business. Thirsk, in Mill St., also advertised a cheap eating house , but it may be that his was of a more temporary nature, opening only for the Show and the Hirings. The pubs too, could be sure of a good trade. By the beginning of July the schedule of prizes was drawn up and the cups, some made by Wilkinson and Kirby, the local jewellers, were on display in the Mechanics' Institute. A prize of £10-10s-0d was given by Count Batthyany to be spent in the shop of a local tradesman.

70

The Show was held in three fields on Beverley Lane belonging to Mrs Kirby of the Bell, to Pickering, the ironfounder and to Jarratt. Mrs Kirby's field contained the large marquee in which she provided the official luncheon for the Society and its 300 guests, headed by the President, Sir Christopher Sykes and his fellow East Riding M.P., Harrison Broadley. The other fields contained the exhibits and "a grandstand filled with a large number of ladies representing the elite of a widely extended district". In the Show, horses had pride of place, but it was noted with satisfaction that all the stock entries were up on previous years, with the exception of pigs. In general terms the Show was said to be the largest for several years with 48 stands of implements, in which a display of churns attracted much attention. The fine display of carriages by Roberts and Stott was also much admired. The weather, which had been threatening all day, held until 4.30 when there was a heavy thunderstorm, but it didn't spoil the rest of the day. It was a tradition for Mrs Kirby to put on an evening entertainment in the marquee. The doors opened at 6.00 p.m., prices 1/- "and 6d for the working class". The bill consisted of The Brothers Elva (celebrated gymnasts), two Australian duettists, Derr Hong (the Indian Club performer), Little Fanny (the Infant Prodigy) and D'Rande and Martin on the horizontal bar. The evening was to end with a Grand Ball in the gas-lit marquee.

The 17th Show was felt to be a success and it is perhaps a measure of the new found confidence of the "resuscitated society" that when Malton was awarded the Yorkshire Show for 1872 and approached Driffield to suspend the local show, the society refused, pointing out that the Quarterly Fairs were now of little importance, that Club Feasts had decayed and it was now only the Show that remained to bring the local community together. They would hold the 18th Show as normal.

CHAPTER EIGHT

AUGUST

On August 12th Thomas Holderness, the editor of the Driffield Observer, wrote a leader entitled 'The Cholera Coming'. There was no immediate justification for it, other than that in previous years Driffield had suffered outbreaks of illness in the summer months. Holderness was writing over twenty years after the link had been established between the spread of cholera and the water supply, but offered little more than well-meaning advice to white-wash the walls of buildings and to indulge in less alcohol. "Perhaps the three most powerful allies that cholera has, are dirt, intemperance and impure water." Driffield had a touching confidence in its water supply in the early 19th Century. Kelly's Directory proclaimed year after year that "the water about Driffield is very good and being unimpregnated with mineral particles, is well calculated for brewing". There was an almost religious belief in the purity of the springs at Cranwell near the centre of the town, "a rude pure spring breaking and bubbling out in several places at once, forming distinct beautiful fountains".The main spring had been enclosed by a square iron tank by 1871. Several local people recalled that a Dr Soffitt had, at some time in the past, pronounced upon the purity of the water and the Driffield Times, elevating him to the "highest authority in the land" claimed Cranwell as "the purest spring in England , the water being almost equal to distilled water".

For those people who were able to afford the cost, water was obtained by boring wells. There were several firms in the town who undertook well-sinking of this kind, including George Wilson , a painter, plumber and decorator on Middle St., whilst ironfounders such as Pickering and Gibson, supplied pumps. A Vestry meeting felt it was the duty of all property owners to put down pumps since there was an excellent supply of pure water within a few feet of the surface in any part of the town. No house, they declared should be left dependent for their water supply on the town's beck. They considered the question of compelling owners to provide pumps, but it is a reflection on the uncertainties of local government in Driffield that they were unclear if the Vestry had the power to do this. [1] There were public water supplies. In addition to Cranwell, there was a walled-in fountain on Bridge St. and a pump in Wrangham Row, one of the poorest areas of the town, but "it was a picture of neglect, dirt and uselessness". There was also a pump, still in existence, on Bridge St, placed at a convenient height for the carts of farmers, "who in droughty summer are constantly leading water for agricultural purposes". Driffield also had a town water cart, driven in 1871 by John Moate of River Head, but what precise function this had, whether it was organised through the Vestry as part of the fire precautions or where it obtained the supply of water, is unclear.

Those sections of society that could rely on wells and pumps were confident in the water supply. They were bolstered in that confidence by Dr Simon, brought in by the Vestry, who confirmed that "the quality of the water so obtained is excellent" and that "all, or nearly all, the old wells in the town have had a casing pipe put in so as to exclude any soakage from the top". He reported that there were few, if any, shallow wells in the town. For those who had no access to pumps, their source of water was, perforce, the beck.

What this meant in practice is best understood by quoting from an article in the Driffield Times, [2] perhaps written in response to a Poor Law Inspector's report on the state of the beck. It seems to be the first public questioning of the water supply as distinct from the sewage question. Jackson began by stating plainly that "the water supply of Driffield is insufficient". "The inhabitants of some houses obtain their supply from a beck which flows through Driffield and receives sewage from several parts of the town." He then traced the water supply through the town from the

73

point where it emerged from the Wolds in "innumerable crystal springs at Waterfalowns" to form the beck. He was conscious of the irony that the despised North Enders "who perhaps have no pumps" had the purest water from "the never failing fountains " of the springs, though the springs were sufficiently distant from the houses at North End to make the purity of the water at the point of extraction more questionable. From North End the stream flowed past Mrs Holtby's brewery, where "it is made available for mechanical purposes" and passed "over a fine silvery bottom" to Bridge St. where it supplied "those who live in that district and have no wells or pumps, with splendid water. Up to this point there is but little or no sewage." Jackson doesn't mention Matthew's artificial manure and chemical works but it is hard to believe, given its situation, that it had no effect on the stream that passed below it. From Bridge St. onwards "there is a great quantity of sewerage; but on the west side of the beck merely irrigates the gardens of the Middle St. inhabitants, whilst on the east side most of the inhabitants either have, or might easily have at a comparatively small cost, pumps put down".

Jackson then paid ritual tribute to "the almost world celebrated Cranwell", but even this "pure nectar of nature" was being polluted by a large amount of sewage flowing from the back premises of the row of large houses in Eastgate. A large drain at the bottom of Hodgson's Lane carried the sewage from Middle St. into the beck and past the gas works, where water was extracted for pumping, before flowing by the cattle market,with all that that implied, and past the bottom of Doctors Lane, Chapel Lane and Brook St. from which "the sewage of each of these, it very necessarily carries off". By that point 'flow' is probably the wrong word to use. Jackson describes the passage down to Albion Mills as a "sluggish, dirty, Styx-like sheet of water with a muddy bed and very often fetid smell, which must prove detrimental to the health of that district and when the water is held up, this bad smell extends even to the Doctors Lane bridge". It is probable that people were still extracting water from the stream below the cattle market. From Albion Mills, the beck struggled under the railway to enter the canal.

Jackson concluded that "the beck can not possibly be dispensed with in carrying off such a vast amount of sewage" but despite the state of the beck, "in other respects there is not a town in England better supplied with purer water". For Jackson, the answer was for house proprietors, who had not put down pumps in the vicinity of the beck, to do so. The responsibility was therefore seen as resting with the individual. The solution of a pure water supply was within the reach of all by sinking wells and putting down pumps and there was felt by most people to be no communal responsibility and therefore no communal cost to be properly borne by ratepayers.

People were fully aware that Driffield had a sewage problem. It was impossible to ignore "the collection of sewage stored up in the beck at the bottom of Brook Street". It was realised in 1870 that the beck was in "a filthy condition and must, with a warm autumn, spread malaria. The water is very low and the sides of the stream are lined with slimy fetid mud". Outbreaks of typhoid in 1867 and scarlet fever in 1868, had resulted in letters to the papers, which advocated building a brick culvert alongside the beck, which would be flushed by diverting the beck into it through a system of 'gates'. An engineer brought in to consider the question of drainage, reported dwellings next to water closets, slaughter houses, pig-sties and privies containing not less than 6" of sewage matter. There were rumours of cholera, "that dreaded foe" in 1871 and fever, typhoid and small-pox were regularly experienced in the town. There had been a public meeting in the Corn Exchange as long ago as 1854 to consider the unsatisfactory state of the town's drainage but whilst the Poor Law authorities could, and did, chase up individuals, these were essentially measures that were peripheral to the problem. Thus, whilst they instructed house-holders to do something about over-flowing privies or gave John Postgate twenty-one days to provide drains for three of his cottages in Little Driffield, or censure John Harker for "again" emptying a tank and allowing the contents to run down Washington St. causing a very offensive nuisance, or drew Mr Holtby's attention to the offensive state of the drain in a field near Bridge St., any real solution to the problem could only be found on a communal basis and that meant a significant charge on the rates. Whilst the principal ratepayers, who attended the Vestry meetings, could feel secure in their pumped water supply and saw no close connection between water and sewage, they preferred to shelve the sewage problem.

It is perhaps significant that that complacency was dented by a letter from Dr. Scotchburn, who, as the Medical Officer for the Poor Law Union, probably had more first hand knowledge of the poorer areas of town than anyone else with medical knowledge. He drew attention to a case of typhoid, caused, he thought, by sewage, poisoning a well which was within three feet of two privies and within five feet of an ash-pit latrine that was only partly roofed. A slimy trickle oozed out of the latrine past the wooden pump case of the well. When the well was opened up, the earth was so impregnated with impurities that the workmen could hardly proceed and when the brickwork was broken through, the rush of fetid gasses was unbearable. Scotchburn pointed out that every member of the family using this water had complained of illness and, in a passage that clearly had a great effect on local public opinion, ended with "a great many of us are at present making tea with boiled diluted sewage as well as washing our hands and faces in it ". Whilst there was undoubted migration of young people into the town, such accounts help to explain why nearly 80% of Driffield's population was below the age of 45 and why there were only 435 people (8.3%) over the age of 60.

Dr Beard's Poor Law inspection of the beck, Jackson's article in the Times and, above all, Scotchburn's letter, had an effect. A series of Vestry meetings early in 1872, set up committees and commissioned reports from engineers. Jennings wanted to establish a water works on a similar basis to the gas works, others discussed a main drain parallel to the beck, but always the question of the cost to the ratepayers rose to delay matters and it was to be 1880 before a sewage outfall works was established at River Head and 1884 before pure water was supplied to the town from the Spellowgate pumping station

Driffield had no local Board of Health in 1871 to regulate conditions and it was left to the Poor Law Guardians to ensure that the law was complied with. At the same time as he drew attention to the state of the beck, Dr Beard pointed to the number of children born in 1871 that had not been vaccinated as the law demanded. Mindful that smallpox was endemic in the district, he recommended that public notices should be put up to remind parents of the requirement of vaccination and that they be required to take their children to stations for inspection and prosecuted in cases of neglect. W.P.Sumner, the Relieving Officer for the Union, was also paid £10 a year as the Presenting Officer under the Vaccination Act and it was no doubt under pressure from Dr Beard and the Guardians that he summoned William Charter for refusing to have his child vaccinated. The heavy fine of 20/- and 18/- costs was no doubt designed to discourage others from refusing.

In 1871 Driffield had five doctors or 1 for every 1054 of the population, but since their services had to be paid for, they were not generally available and the imposing houses of Dr Scotchburn and Dr Fortune, standing side-by-side in Middle St., is evidence that most of their patients were not poor. Both were well qualified. Scotchburn, a local man, was the Medical Officer for the Poor Law Union, a part-time post for which he was paid £41 a year, which meant that his services were more widely available than those of the others, though it is clear that all the local doctors willingly gave their services at accidents and crises. Dr John Fortune, a 50 year old Scot, was the best qualified. Having studied as a doctor, he became a member of the Royal College of Surgeons at Edinburgh and a Licenciate of the Apothecaries' Company in London. Dr

Eames was active in Driffield in 1871, but doesn't appear in the census, though he was living in Middle St. in 1872. Dr Richard Wood, possibly the son of a Middleton doctor, and Dr Thomas Britton, aged 35, from Bradford, were the other two general practitioners. Britton employed a young medical assistant and like Scotchburn, had a lunatic living with him in New Rd., presumably giving asylum to an individual whose family could afford to pay for private care. Less fortunate perhaps, were the twelve mentally handicapped, who were resident in the workhouse and for whom no separate provision was made. The Poor Law Guardians did make genuine attempts to help individuals. Thirteen year old Sarah Sellers, blind from birth, was found a place in York School for the Blind, but unable to wash or dress herself, she was removed at the request of the York school authorities, who felt she was incapable of benefitting from the training they offered. She was eventually found a place at Bath Institute for the Blind at a cost of £12 a year. [3] The Guardians were also conscientious enough to visit Clifton asylum in 1871 to review the conditions of local patients placed there, perhaps motivated by the knowledge that the East Riding Justices were opening their own county asylum in 1871 and that there was to be a special county rate to fund it.[4]

The census enumerators were asked to record those who were blind and who were deaf and dumb. It's clear that this was not always done conscientiously. John Lill, who was disfigured by the acid, is not listed as blind, but for what the figures are worth, nine people are recorded, including John Tindall, an ex-pupil of the Wilberforce School for the Blind, who was appointed organist at the Parish Church and played at most of the town's social functions. The eccentricities of the census are shown by the decision of Solomon Parker to take it upon himself to record those who were paralysed, of which there were five in the section of the town for which he was responsible, in addition to the solitary deaf-mute in Driffield.

There were no resident dentists in the town,but

every market day several attended in local shops to pull teeth and replace them with sets of false teeth at £5 or 5/- a tooth, complete with gold clasp. Only one dentist offered the incentive of nitrous oxide. There were several local chemists and druggists. Elgey, Sterriker, Parkinson and Bordass provided ointments and medicines and in the latter case "Bordass' restorative balm for the growth of hair". The local papers were full of adverts for quack remedies that could be sent for. Wrangham's pills sold at $7\frac{1}{2}$d a box and cured amongst other things, loss of appetite, sickness, giddiness, headache, spasms and liver complaints. The liver was a constant source of concern but Dr King's dandelion and quinine pills at least promised to sooth it without resorting, as was more common, to mercury. For those who suffered from 'nervous disability', the coded reference in Victorian papers for all sexual diseases and problems, 'The Secret Friend' was available by post to guide 'nervous sufferers' in self-medication.

Driffield had been fortunate to have a Cottage Hospital since 1867. It was based in a house in Brook St. that had been loaned by a well-wisher, but which was reclaimed in 1871. The management committee of ladies led by Mrs Reynard of Sunderlandwick, Miss Sykes and Mrs Matthews, the Honorary Secretary, determined to build a new hospital. Their annual report in 1871 showed that the existing six bed hospital had admitted 45 in-patients of whom only 2 had died. 22 were pronounced cured and 18 relieved. In addition they had treated 59 out-patients. They employed a full-time nurse at Brook St., whilst Dr Britton acted as the Honorary Medical Officer. He recieved much praise for successfully operating on a man to remove a collar bone, a long and painful operation presuming the absence of anaesthetic. The running costs of the hospital were in the order of £130 a year, which were met by subscriptions, donations and by payments from patients of 1/6d a week. The financing of a new hospital was a considerable undertaking, but it was well supported in the town, and the Beverley architect, William Hawe, was commissioned to design it for a site on Nafferton Road. By August

1871 he was asking builders to submit tenders for a building which was to include a men's day ward, a women's day ward, a sick room, an operating room, a nurses' and board room and a kitchen. The hospital, which was to become known later as 'Ten Gables' was a major asset to the town, but the 1871 Annual Report noted that amongst the labourers "a little hesitation still exists to avail themselves of the hospital when injured, although admission is free and immediate in any case of accident". If respectability was one watchword of Victorian society, independence was another. A distrust of charity and a reliance on one's own resources in a spirit of self-help, were seen as the necessary attributes of both respectability and independence.

REFERENCES
1. Driffield Times : 4/5/1872
2. Ibid: 23/3/1872
3. H.C.R.O. : P.U.D. 20/10/70 and 13/6/72
4. Ibid 29/6/71

CHAPTER NINE

SEPTEMBER

By the last week of August, the harvest was being gathered in. It was an operation that was to last all through September to the harvest thanksgiving service on September 27th and was the climax of the farming year. Driffield's open fields had been enclosed in 1742, one hundred and thirty years before, but there were still echoes of the past in the Driffield of 1871. There were still two farm complexes in the town itself, a reminder of the time when, as in most Wold villages, the farm houses stood in the main street. John Wilson farmed 136 acres from his farmhouse in Eastgate and it was on Mary England's 90 acre farm based on Middle St., that William Adams lost his foot and, in the end, his life, in the accident with the thrashing machine during the harvest. Driffield still had a pinder, Moses Leadbeater, though the pound was overgrown with trees and bushes. It is by no means clear which body appointed him and it wasn't clear to contemporaries what his powers were. In June 1871, Robert Ness of Spellowgate Farm, left his pony tethered in Spellowgate and was annoyed to find that Moses Leadbeater had impounded it. After a heated argument, Ness released the animal, but was taken to court by the pinder, who claimed his 1/- fee. The Justices were obviously bemused by this and tried to throw light on what basis the 1/- fee was arrived at, finally giving up and declaring it to be "the law of Moses". A further echo of the past was that the triangular shaped three acre field at the south-west corner of Cross Trods was still known in 1871 as 'amen corner' because, 130 years before, it had been awarded to the parish clerk by the enclosure commissioners in recognition of his duties.[1]

There were a number of farms cum smallholdings in the immediate vicinity of the town that were worked in conjunction with some other occupation. John Dunn, a timber merchant, had 30 acres at the corner of Dunn's Lane, whilst Henry Marshall, the corn miller at King's Mill also had the additional income from 40 acres. Norwood Rams farmed 26 acres near Westgate, whilst William Lidster and Robert Ness had 29 acres and 11 acres on Spellowgate. The larger farms, at the edge of the parish, ranged in size from 700 acres at Danesdale and 600 acres at the Wold farm (now Wold House farm) down to Field House farm on Nafferton Rd. at 360 acres. This represented a significant increase in acreage in the previous hundred years since the largest farm on the lord of the manor's estate in 1774 was 287 acres. This can only have come about by the amalgamation of smaller farms.

The pattern of working the farms has been well described by local farm workers relating their experiences at the beginning of the 20th Century. [2] In 1871 four of the six largest farms had a workforce of nine men living-in. Danesdale had eleven and Field House five. These would be supplemented by weekly labourers hired from among the 153 agricultural labourers who lived in Driffield and by day labourers brought in, not just for the harvest, but for jobs such as hoeing turnips. On the smaller farms, the foreman might live in a farm cottage and eat in the farm house, but often on the larger farms, the Hind-Foreman had a separate Hind House, where his wife provided board for the live-in labourers out of an allowance agreed with the farmer. She might be helped by the wife of one of the labourers. The chief horseman on the farm was the Waggoner, followed by 'Thoddy' and 'Fowaty', the third and fourth men after the foreman and the waggoner. Each man normally had a lad to work with him, the 'least lad' being attached to Fowaty. It was recognised that a man and a boy should be responsible for a maximum of six horses, with a work force of about eighteen horses on a 500 acre farm. A shepherd with his lad and a beastman might make up the labour force, though there was often a groom, responsible directly to the farmer, or 'gaffer', for the farm horses from foaling to being broken-in.

This pattern can be seen in the example of Middlefield farm of 400 acres, where George Dunning was the 'gaffer'. The foreman, or 'Boss', was a 51 year old widower, Thomas Stephenson, which presumably meant that the men ate in the farm house, presided over by Dunning's married sister, who acted as his housekeeper with the aid of a 19 year old maid. There were five live-in labourers, with ages ranging from 21 to 14, plus the shepherd, Richard Pickering, a married man of 56. Danesdale and Great Kendale were farmed by two brothers, William and James Allanson, originally from Setterington. Both were considerable households. James Allanson had five of his children living with him and two grand-children. They had a nurse and two domestic maids, alongside a groom, a shepherd and six farm labourers, the two youngest being only 12 years old. Danesdale had twenty-one people, family and workers, living-in. The Wold farm had three shepherds in addition to the six live-in workers.

Clearly the weather was all important in relation to the harvest. A period of copious rain early in June was followed by a cold spell, but early in July the papers were reporting that the crops were "healthy and promising" but would need a month to mature. By late July, Turner was advertising his stock of harvest ale at a 1/- a gallon. A period of "brilliant weather" in August meant that the reapers went into the fields with scythes to open out the corn field, by cutting an area large enough for the mechanical reaper to be set up. They then cut a border around the field by hand, wide enough for the horses pulling the reaper to work without treading the uncut crop. The harvest bell was rung from the church at 5 a.m.and again at 7.00 in the evening to mark the hours of labour throughout the harvest 'month', though even in 1871 this was something of an anachronism. Nevertheless by August 26th the Driffield Times could report that the harvest was in full swing. Once the field had been opened up with the scythe, "the reaping machine is quietly walking round 20, 30, 40 acre fields". Harvest, it was reported had "lost much of the poetry of former years ......the whet and sough of the scythe has given place to that monster worker, the reaping machine". Nostalgia is not a modern phenomenen.

"The monster worker" may have cut the crop effectively, but it still had to be gathered into sheaves, tied and placed in stooks to dry and this was very labour intensive. Labour in 1871 was scarce. The Driffield Times blamed the introduction of machinery, which had "almost stopped the influx of Irish and distant labour" but it is doubtful if this was indeed the case. Certainly there was evidence of Irish harvest workers celebrating enthusiastically enough to come before the courts, but whatever the cause, it was reported that on some farms, the corn was cut but laid just as the reaper left it, it having been impossible to find labour to tie it up. The wages of the temporary workers were high. John Readman was paid 18/- a week plus his meat, for a month from August 23rd, though it didn't stop him from absconding.

Whatever the labour problems, the corn had to be carried home once it was sufficiently dry and stacked in quantities that would provide sufficient work for one day's thrashing, thus making the most efficient use of the steam thrashing machine, which was cumbersome and difficult to manoeuvre. The wheat stack was usually placed as near the granary as possible , since the wheat was carried from the machine in 18 stone bags. Oats, carried in 12 stone sacks, could be stacked further away.î(3)ï Thrashing needed a workforce of ten to fork the sheaves from the stack on to the machine, to feed the corn into the machine, to carry the grain in sacks into the granary and to carry away the chaff, a job usually given to the youngest and least senior lads and considered to be the most unpleasant of the tasks during threshing.[4]

Farmers prospered in the decades before 1871. They benefitted from the steady increase in the population, which ensured an expanding home market largely free from foreign competition. By 1871 the railway network had developed to an extent that allowed them to reach markets well beyond the reach of their fore-fathers and a prosperous middle class meant that there was a constant demand for farm produce in the ever-expanding towns. Mrs Beeton's 'Book of Household Management' and a 'Dictionary of Everyday Cookery' were on sale at Jackson's for 7/6d and 3/6d and reflected the rising standard of living of at least some sections of society. Nevertheless, it is possible with the benefit of hindsight, to look at the farming situation in Driffield in 1871 and see the tell-tale signs that were to point to the agricultural depression of the last quarter of the 19th Century.

The September sheep fairs had always been an important feature of the Driffield farming calendar. Earlier in the year it had been noted at the Easter fair that sheep were more expensive because over the last two years lambs had been killed in "extraordinary numbers to meet the deficiency of horned cattle". The deficiency was caused by cattle plague, which had been present on the Wolds for at least two years to a degree that was proving serious. Moves were taken to prevent it spreading. In October a cattle inspector brought a Sledmere dealer to court for selling a beast with the plague to a Driffield butcher. The fine of £3 reflected the alarm. Early in 1872 the cattle market was closed and the Vestry appointed an assessor to value the animals slaughtered with the disease. In the short run the disease led to an increased demand for sheep at the September fairs especially as there was a plentiful supply of turnips on which to feed them over the winter. Prices were high. At the first of the fairs, 5000 lambs were on offer at between 38/- and 50/-, whilst 500 grazing ewes reached £3 a head. At the later fair on September 19th some 6000 sheep were on offer at similar prices, with rams at £7-£8 a head. Few cattle were for sale, but a limited supply of in-calvers sold at £17-£25 a head. The Driffield Times reported in pessimistic tones that "meat is dear already, as many a pinched family knows too well". It was not just meat. Local cow-keepers raised the cost of milk from 3d a qt. to 4d. Worse was to follow, for foot and mouth was discovered

85

in seven animals pastured in a field on Wansford Rd., spread, it was thought, from a fair at Malton. There were other outbreaks in Kilham and Nafferton. Any initial advantage farmers derived from higher prices was soon more than lost by the decimation of herds and flocks. The paper's pessimism continued. "There is no longer much room to doubt that to the misfortunes of a deficient harvest will be added this season the disaster of a cattle plague."

The most significant pointer to a worsening situation however was to be found in the adverts of two local grocers, Henry Angas and Thomas Raylor, who were selling 4 lb. and 6 lb. tins of Australian mutton and beef. The meat came from Australia packed in large iron cases holding about 2½ tons. "Sheep are packed whole, without bone, and cured and when the iron case is filled with the meat, boiling fat is run into the case, which is then hermetically sealed." Unappetising as this sounds, Angas listed eight advantages to persuade people to buy, claiming it to be superior to English meat, "tender, sweet and sound" though "somewhat overdone". It was the fact that it could be sold for 8d a lb., "cheaper by more than one half than English meat" that was the crucial point. The opening of the Suez canal cut a month off the journey from Australia and that, together with improving techniques for preserving food, meant that farmers were not as protected from foreign competition as in the 1850's and 60's. The development of railways across the prairies of Canada and the U.S.A. would soon leave British farmers vulnerable to imports of American wheat and a catastrophic fall in British wheat prices. Few Driffield farmers contemplating the harvest in September 1871, could have forseen the difficult times that lay ahead for them.

There were other harvest celebrations in September. There had been a Driffield Floral and Horticultural Society for some years, but though still in existence, it was moribund and a new organisation, with the same title, was formed in 1871, to try to breathe new life into the old society. A new committee was formed with Richard Davison as the secretary, and a

sub-committee of Matthews, Jackson and Teale opened
negotiations with the old society "to try to merge plans
with the new movement". When they were repulsed, they
decided to go ahead independently and to hold a Grand
Exhibition on Friday, September 8th. Almost at the last
moment, it was decided to extend the show from being an
exhibition of plants, flowers and fruits to include a
dog show. They turned out to be the stars, attracting no
fewer than 322 entries in 15 classes. It was said to be
Driffield's first ever dog show and was an undoubted
success. The Grand Exhibition was held in Mrs Kirby's
show field and whilst attempts were made to open up the
classes to all sections of society, by including
'cottagers' classes' for the best baked bread, for
vegetables, plants and flowers, it's clear that the
society was aimed mainly at the gentry and the more
affluent middle classes, who had the benefit of
conservatories, glass-houses and professional gardeners.
There were classes for apricots, nectarines, peaches,
melons, white and black grapes, figs, gooseberries, red
and black currants, pears and apples.

Mrs Kirby's field was in use again the
following day when the National school held an afternoon
of wheel-barrow races, sack-jumping, flat races and
cricket for the pupils, under the watchful eye of the
new schoolmaster, Mr Santon. The National School
managers then went to inspect the new schoolroom in
Harland Lane that Jarratt was persisting in establishing
at his own expense, in face of the opposition from the
rest of the School Board.

Despite the pressures of the harvest, some
people found time to take advantage of railway
excursions to Whitby Show at the end of August and to
Doncaster races in September. Such excursions were not
cheap. Whitby cost 2/6d return and Doncaster 10/- first
class and 5/6d second class, the train departing from
the sidings, under the clock of the Linseed Oil Company
building. The N.E.R. took care to confirm that the
second class passengers would have covered stock and not
open carriages.

A rival attraction was the performance of W.S. Woodin at the Assembly Rooms, who promised a one-man show in which he played fifty characters, male and female, including a dining room scene in which he played three characters at once. His show was well received by the Driffield Times, which reported that he "seemed almost possessed of ubiquity, his transitions from place to place were so rapid and the transformations so suddenly effected." The performance of Sam Bayliss, who brought his puppet show of French Marionettes to the same stage, had Holderness of the Observer, "splitting his sides with laughter at the clown, gazing with delight into Aladins's garden and the Babes in the Wood", but not all such entertainments were well received. The original and only Female Christy's Minstrel Troup's appearance at the Exchange was "a most miserable affair" of only one hour, including a ten minute interval. The star performer, "the two-headed Nightingale", engaged "at fabulous cost" was, not for the first time, "unavoidably prevented from being in attendance". Of the four female and one male in the Female Troup, there was "not one amongst them who could sing a song decently, neither had they any good jokes". Several parties from the country demanded their money back and the Observer concluded that it would be as well if Christy's Troup did not return.

REFERENCES

1 Driffield Express 1872
2 See :- Day : Horses on the Farm : Hutton Press 1981
    and Reffold : Pie for Breakfast : Hutton Press 1984
3 Reffold p82
4 Ibid p56

CHAPTER TEN

OCTOBER

Mrs Selina Coleman was a 38 year old widow, living in a two roomed house in Washington Street. She kept herself and her four children by working at night as a laundress taking in washing and ironing and as a charwoman by day. Her youngest child, an eleven month old baby, had whooping cough and couldn't sleep. Mrs Coleman, having spent all night ironing, laid on the bed beside it to comfort the child and get it off to sleep. She fell asleep. The laundry, airing in front of the fire downstairs, caught fire and the house was in flames. The whole family suffered burns before they could be rescued, two so severely, that it was thought at first, that they would not survive.

In October, Ann Wardell, a 14 year old girl, complained to the police that her father had attempted to rape her. The Driffield Observer decided that the "particulars (of the case) are not fit for publication" and the magistrates in sentencing Charles Wardell to six months in the House of Correction "could not but blush to think that there was such a man in the East Riding".

It was in October too, that 31 year old Elizabeth Grasby realised, as the Hirings approached, that she would not be retained in her present position. She took laudanum and a 3d packet of Battle's vermin destroyer bought from Parkinson's the chemists and had to have her stomach cleaned out four times. She had been employed as the housekeeper at Field House farm, where the farmer was Thomas Craven, a 27 year old bachelor. She had been seduced by Craven "who had alluded to marriage all the year, but had deceived her and turned her out of a place". As her year's employment came up for renewal, she realised the situation and attempted suicide. As Craven said in evidence "she wanted to stay on; I gave her notice to leave and she was very much distressed to go home (to Hotham), not having a place to go to". Attempted suicide was a criminal offence. The magistrates treated the case humanely, giving a "kind, yet firm reproof" to Grasby and a public rebuke to Craven. "He had done a very serious and wicked thing to the young woman and hoped he would make compensation." They then ordered him to pay the costs of the case. It is impossible to quarrel with the justice of this, but from a legal point of view, no matter how badly he had behaved, Craven had not committed any offence and was not being charged before the court. It perhaps reflects the way in which J.P.'s could behave in a very high-handed manner because of their standing in society.

Clearly it would be wrong to project these three examples as typical of the condition of women in Driffield in 1871. Not all domestic servants were sexually exploited and not all children abused. At the same time it is probable that their experience was not unique and it is difficult not to imagine that other women, struggling to bring up families by laundering, were not as hard pressed as Selina Coleman. The two tables in the appendix are worth close study. They show the occupations of all working women in Driffield and the age pattern of marriage related to the number of children in the family. From them, it is possible to deduce a pattern of experience that may not be too far removed from that of many women in the town in 1871.

75% of the 209 girls aged under 20, who were working in the town, were domestic servants. Two, Elizabeth Cornforth and Anne Shores, were eleven years old and there were seven girls aged twelve in full-time employment. Nearly 16% of the houses in Driffield had at least one domestic servant living-in and sixty-one houses had two or more. In addition there were a number of domestic servants who did not live-in, 55 in total. If it can be presumed that some of these girls worked in houses where there were no resident staff, then perhaps 18-19% is a realistic assessment of households with servants in 1871.

The only other significant area of employment open to young girls seeking work was in the various

91

branches of dressmaking and millenery, which absorbed 33 girls. In all 123 women, 20% of the female working population, were engaged in the trade, a figure which is not too surprising given that all clothes and hats were hand made. Fawcett employed a few girls as book-binders and book-colourers, illuminating the prints, and Taylor's sewing machine company absorbed a handful, but the vast majority of girls entered domestic service and remained there until their twenties.The table in the appendix shows the marital state of all women between the age of 16 and 45, together with the number of children in the family. It is clear from the table that it was unusual for women to marry before the age of 22. Out of the 271 women between the ages of 16 and 21 only twenty-two (8%) were married and it is necessary to look at 24 year olds before the majority of women in any one year group are married. The sharp fall in the number of domestic servants aged 30 plus reflects the pattern of marriage in the mid-twenties, at which point they left employment. Those who were still in work were likely to be in the post of house-keeper or cook, as was the case of Elizabeth Grasby at Field House.

Once married, the ever expanding columns showing the number of children in the family as the age of the women increases, tells its own story of large families and years of child-bearing, but it needs to be realised that the figures only reveal the number of children alive and living at home in April 1871. Several of the women over 40 were likely to have had additional children who were old enough to have left home and the table can not show the number of children who had died. Given the state of the water supply and the crowded living conditions, infant mortality must have been high. The figures therefore do not reveal the number of pregnancies that a woman marrying in her early twenties could expect. The tables also reveal that a proportion of women could expect to be widowed at an early age, but again the figures underestimate this factor since they fail to include those widows who remarried.

It is not really possible to form an accurate picture of the illegitimacy rates in Driffield from the census, but the inquest on Sarah West's illegitimate daughter, Alice, is revealing about the situation. Sarah West lived in Dobson's Buildings in Westgate. She, her sister, three brothers and a friend, Jessy Potts, slept in one room with the baby. She had gone into the workhouse to give birth to the child, but left immediately after. The child quickly became ill. West "thought it had the belly-ache. It would not take the breast" and she had given it some "white mixture from Elgey's, some boiled bread and biscuit etc.". The baby had died soon afterwards. The workhouse medical officer expressed his concern at the inquest about the number of women who came into the workhouse to give birth, left almost immediately and then placed the child out with a woman to nurse it, where it died shortly afterwards. Sarah West had lost a child the year before in such circumstances. [1] There were hints in the medical officer's evidence that infanticide could not be entirely discounted. A similar case, also in 1868, was revealed by the inquest on three month old Jane Bower, the illegitimate daughter of a domestic servant, who had placed the child with Martha Watson as soon as it was born. Mrs Watson was paid 3/- a week to look after it but "it was a cross child", it had "grown but little and was very small". The doctor found it "extremely emaciated, skin and bone and no flesh .....(with) ulceration on various parts of the body". The verdict was death by natural causes.

The magistrates usually awarded maintenance of 1/6d a week for the upkeep of illegitimate children, though as always they were capable of applying the law in their own fashion. Rachel Butterworth applied for an affiliation order against the father of her illegitimate daughter. The case was not disputed, but the J.P.'s, on learning that this was not her first child, decided that "in order to record their sense of disapproval of such kind of immorality, they had come to a determination to allow only 1/- per week instead of 1/6d for a second child". No doubt the Nafferton labourer, who had fathered the child, was grateful to the bench for their stand against immorality.

The opportunities for employment for women once married, were very limited. Dressmakers and seamstresses could work from home and in the 30-50 age range, they represent the largest single group, but as the age range increases, so does the number of women who survived like Selina Coleman, by taking in laundry or by opening up their homes to lodgers. A fortunate few earned a living as shopkeepers, such as Martha Houghey, who had the Berlin Wool and Fancy Repositry in New Rd. or Eleanor Bookless, who ran the Refreshment Rooms in Middle Street. Both of these ladies were widows. No fewer than seven of these pubs were run by women at the time of the census and this figure does not include Mrs Kirby, who seems to have been in all contemporary references, the driving force behind the Bell, whilst her son followed his own profession of auctioneer. She was absent on census day. The ladies who ran a 19th Century pub can not have faced an easy task. All were widows. The 66 year old Elizabeth England must have been a formidable lady to have made a success of running the Bay Horse, situated as it was in "one of the dark places of the earth", North End.

A glance down the list of occupations seems to show a number of women successfully running businesses as brewers, brick and tile manufacturers and wholesale grocers. Closer inspection however, nearly always shows that this is only the accidental spotlight of the census on one particular moment of time. Thus Jane Turner at 35, seems from the census to be the model of a successful business woman, employing eighteen men in an enterprise that included a brick and tile manufactury, a brewery and a wine and spirits retailers. In fact she had been widowed shortly before the census and her 20 year old step-son advertised soon afterwards that he would be running the business that his grandfather had started. A similar example might be Hannah Lance, who in the census employed six men and ran a wholesale grocery business in a substantial commercial building in Middle Street. The reality was that her husband had died at the end of 1870, but in her case there was no obvious figure to take over the firm and it is possible that she ran the business herself, since in both the 1872 and the 1879 directories, the firm is listed under her name. Mary Holtby's brewery was in her name, but at 69, it is more likely that her son, who managed the brewery for her, had the dominant voice in its running. Similarly, the farmer, Mary England, had her son living with her and he presumably ran the farm on a day to day basis.

In one sense however, the table of female occupations clearly underestimates the role of women in 1871, since nearly all of the small shops in the town, which appear in the census under the male head of household, appear in reality, to have been run by the wives, whilst the husbands sought work elsewhere, either as the family's main source of income, or to supplement the income from the shop. Thirsk, the grocer on the corner of Cross Hill, who worked full time as a solicitor's clerk and Temple, the shopkeeper who was crushed by the boiler, have already been noted as examples of the trend, but another typical example is Rhoda Appleby, who ran a grocery shop in Middle St., whilst her husband worked as a joiner. It is impossible to know to what extent these women simply served behind the counter or organised the business to a greater extent.

The list of female occupations is misleading in one other sense. The 30 year old Elizabeth Lindsey, who gave her occupation as a silk weaver was one of three unattached women at Berriman's brothel at North End. She and Elizabeth Evans both hailed from Lancashire and the occupation of hawker that the latter gave to the census enumerator was probably more accurate. The third woman, from Scotland, gave no occupation. There may incidentally be a family tradition in Berriman's occupation, as a Mrs Berriman ran a brothel described as "a great nuisance to the area and dishonour to the town" in the 1840's in Brook Street. The police largely ignored prostitution unless the woman, like Matilda Duglass, "a dissipated prostitute" was making a nuisance of herself through drink, or unless a disturbance was involved as when James Bradley went with police to Berriman's and forced an entry, claiming his wife was being detained there. He

95

found her in bed with one of the lodgers and the
resulting fracas spilled over into the street and drew
such "a large concourse of people that it blocked the
street".

For many women old age offered a bleak
prospect.It is true that many lived as part of an
extended family with sons or daughters, perhaps
overcrowded but cared for. Over 10% of Driffield houses
had three or more generations within the same house and
10% had other relations, sisters, nephews etc.,living
with them.For some older women survival was possible by
opening up their homes to lodgers. 74 year old Elizabeth
Shepherdson of Brook St. kept home for a labourer and a
schoolmaster. She was not alone, a total of 141 houses
in Driffield had lodgers. There was a charity which
provided houses for widows. These alms houses were
situated next to the Methodist chapel in Westgate, but
only three of the eight houses were occupied. It is
probable that these were associated with a sum of money
left in Gray's will of 1797 for the upkeep of the "widow
houses". They were already old in 1797 and this may well
account for five of the houses being empty. For many
women the workhouse loomed in old age.

The presence of nephews and neices in the
households of relatives, no doubt reflects the way many
children lost one or both parents at an early age. Life
for many children was hard. Ten year old Robert
Wadsworth, who was brought before the court as
destitute, was found sleeping rough in the brick kilns
and in out-houses. A number of lads who had been begging
at the back doors of houses for a period of 2-3 weeks
after Christmas, were brought before the court by Sgt
Wood on vagrancy charges. The attitude of the courts to
such cases depended on whether they perceived a criminal
offence. Where they did, the bench dealt harshly with
offenders, sentencing the beggers to 21 days hard labour
at the House of Correction. Robert Wadsworth and boys
like him, who were seen as destitute rather than yet
criminal, were often sent to the 'Southampton', a 50 gun
wooden frigate beached in the Humber since 1868 and used
as a training ship to prepare boys for the sea. There

were 184 boys under Capt. Pollard in 1871, many sent by Justices, who saw it as an alternative to the workhouse or to the reformatory. Capt. Pollard remarked optimistically on "the avidity for a sailor's life shown by most of the lads sent to the 'Southampton'". One wonders how long it took ten year old Robert Wadsworth to take to the sea. Interestingly the managers of the 'Southampton' tried to claim maintenance from the newly formed School Board for two Driffield boys sent by the Justices to the hulk.

Some children were in the workhouse because one or both parents were there. The workhouse master frequently advertised "strong boys to be hired as farm servants". Perhaps one was Richard Foster, hired out to a Tibthorpe farmer to work for him until Martinmas for £6. He returned 'home' in February severely bruised. His mother in the workhouse, took the case to court to seek redress. The court was less than sympathetic. Hodgson, one of the Poor Law Guardians, gave evidence that the Board "had given the lad a good rig-out" and claimed "that an occasional flogging for refractory boys did a power of good". The Justices confirmed that Richard Foster had to stay at the farm until "his term of servitude" expired and reminded him that his wages would then be due to the workhouse Guardians.

There were boys in Driffield in full-time work as errand boys from the age of 10, farm boys and telegraph boys aged 12, as well as girls working as servants from the age of 11. Many children worked on the fields long before they took up full-time employment. 'Nottingham Jack' and gang masters like him, negotiated with local farmers from his beer house on Wansford Rd., to supply gangs of children to work on such jobs as potato planting, brassacking, turnip hoeing and potato harvesting. Local evidence was given to the Royal Commission in 1867 that "from the middle of May to the end of July children ....are employed in the fields ...... during this time they lose most of the knowledge which they have acquired previously at school". As a result of that Royal Commission, the Gangs Act of 1867 laid down that no child under 8 was to work and then only in single sexed gangs. The gang masters were to be licensed by local J.P's, often themselves land-owners. The improvements were only marginal. Few gangs had used children under eight. "The little ones under 10 or 11 are not much good as they can not do a good day's work", said Mrs Fergusson to the Royal Commission. John Adams was paying his gang 10d a day and 'Nottingham Jack' 5/- a week at the time of the Commission. [2] As the Driffield Times pointed out in 1870, "only those who live in the country, really know the fearful effects of putting lads of 8 or 10 to exhaustive field labour".

There were homes in Driffield where these sorts of pressures were unknown. The bachelor, Count Batthyany, had a household of 8 servants, a butler, cook, two grooms, a footman, page, a housemaid and kitchen maid. Jennings' two children had a private tutor in a household with five servants. There were 16 households with three or more servants. The more affluent of the middle classes lived comfortably, surrounded by the trappings of Victorian prosperity, but there can have been few homes in Driffield that were not fully aware that family life could be unexpectedly curtailed.

REFERENCES

1 Driffield Times : August 29th 1868
2 Royal Commission on the Employment of Women, Young Persons and Children in Agriculture : 1867 : Minutes of evidence p381

CHAPTER ELEVEN

NOVEMBER

November 5th fell on Sunday in 1871 to the relief of some of the more nervous citizens. The church bells were uncharacteristically silent and the day passed off quietly. Nevertheless the Superintendent of Police issued his annual warning, printed in red letters, not to use firearms, light bonfires, firecrackers or cannons. Any hopes that Gunpowder Plot would pass off peaceably that year were dispelled on the Monday when "the smouldering ashes of youthful ardour blazed forth, guns, cannons, revolvers were fired, bonfires from all quarters illumined the otherwise dark clouds, tar barrels were lighted by invisible hands. Sorties were made by the police, who were diverted from one place to another and it took them all their time to quench the burning tar barrels." The Observer agreed that "the day has only been one of riot and uproar" but felt "the ridiculous practice of commemorating the anniversary seems somewhat on the wane and it is a pity that it is not entirely discontinued. Few people know, or care to know, the history of the time in which it originated."

"The riot and uproar" was to some extent licensed by tradition on Guy Fawkes day but it was never too far below the surface at other times of the year. The General Election of 1868 coincided with the Martinmas holiday. About mid-day a mob took control of the streets, smashed the windows of the Falcon and the Cross Keys, where one of the Tory candidates was staying, dragged "the golden cannister" from above Rawlinson's shop, the Conservative party base, and "kicked it up and down the street from the station to the church and back again". The local police were driven from the street by cobbles and stones, whilst magistrates and the candidate tried to calm the crowd from the balcony of the Bell and swore in special constables, but it needed a reinforcement of police by the 5.30 train to restore order.

The 1871 Hirings were fixed for Monday 13th, which turned out to be a clear frosty morning and a day of bright sun. They were always one of the highlights of the year, the only time when a hired man could legally leave his employment and the time when a farmworker was paid for his previous year's work, entering the farmhouse in strict order of seniority to receive his wages and perhaps agree terms for the following year. Even if the present job was to their liking, the workers would attend the Hirings. It was the start of the one and only week's holiday and an opportunity to see family and friends, who might be on farms too distant to be visited at other times of the year. It was a time to buy boots and clothes for the following year and to put money into the Driffield Savings Bank, which added interest to existing savings in November and took £1271-12s-3d in deposits that week. It was an opportunity to parade the town's streets, to buy Martinmas presents, ear-rings, scarf pins, watchguards or lockets from Boak's Fancy Repository and to admire the special displays of horse brasses in Lundy's and Pinkney's the saddlers, to drink in the pubs and perhaps settle some old scores with unpopular superiors in the yards behind them, to eat in the Eating Houses and Refreshment Rooms and to visit the side-shows at the fair.

The roads into town were crowded fron dawn. First "the cavalcade of the upper section of male servants, the foremen and second chaps, mounted on well-fed draught horses". Then "the carriers' carts, omnibuses and all kinds of vehicles from cabs down to hand carts". Next the early morning trains arrived and "the streets were filled with a dense surging tide of happy humanity". Employers and their wives were also in town, some seeking workers. Male workers stood in the Market Place to negotiate terms, to compare billets and swap experiences with other workers and, if the negotiations were successful, to accept the 'fest' sealing the bargain for the coming year. Girls and women were hired in the Corn Exchange and the Assembly Rooms, a change which was widely regarded with approval as " a few years since, female servants had to herd like cattle in the market place, exposed not only to the pitiless severities of rain and hail and snow, but also to the filthy language and rude conduct of the men servants". They may have been protected from the weather, but one observer recalled that "farmers would pat young women on their shoulders and gauge the width of their stout arms, as though examining a cow in a cattle show".[1] The churches too were active in the Corn Exchange, selling Bibles and Prayer Books and distributing tracts in the street.

There were plenty of opportunities after being hired to spend the 'fest' on the side-shows. Pinfold Place was "literally crowded with places of amusement; wild beasts tame as domestic cats, boxing establishments, learned ponies, which would unheasitatingly tell any love-stricken maiden the name of her future husband, automaton elephants and self-moving wheel barrows ......amusing rat-eaters, shooting galleries and strength indicators". [2] All "did a pretty good stroke of business". For those workers not staying in Driffield it was necessary to move on and the Times noted "the immense pressure at the railway station on Monday night".

One alternative to employment locally was to consider the adverts in the local papers for Otago and Queensland. The 'Jessie Redman' of 1000 tons was scheduled to sail to New Zealand offering assisted passages to agricultural labourers, shepherds, tradesmen, fishermen and female domestic servants. Queensland offered 40 acres of land per adult to those paying their own passage and assisted passages to others. Female domestic servants "for whom there is great demand" were offered a free passage. George Jackson acted as the agent from his shop in Exchange Street. The editor of the Observer encouraged emigration, especially to Canada, in a series of leaders throughout the year. He saw emigration as the answer to many problems at home. "There is no danger of there being any unreasonable drain of our working classes from the old world to the new. .... A large proportion (i.e. the poor) are poor from their own faults; from idleness, improvidence and drunkenness." The solution he felt was emigration.

The 1871 Hirings were accounted a success "and good wages were obtained". They do however, illustrate the difficulty of attempting to gain a clear impression of wage levels in 1871. Wages and prices have been quoted quite deliberately throughout this account to try to establish a relationship and a sense of how families lived. The difficulties may be gauged from the reports in the two local newspapers of the wages negotiated at the Hirings. Both editors were experienced and in a position to know, yet quote very different figures. The Times reported foremen being paid £15-£20 a year and some as high as £25. The Observer said foremen received £25-£30. Waggoners £12-£14 in the Times; £18-£22 in the Observer. Young lads £6-£8 in the Times; ploughboys £11-£12 in the Observer. The Times gives fuller figures for female servants, quoting £17-£20 for cooks, £10-£13 for housemaids, £8-£10 for kitchen maids and £8-£12 for general servants. The Observer simply reported that kitchen girls to upper servants received £10-£15 a year.

Given such conflicting evidence, it is clearly very difficult to establish with any degree of certainty any general picture of wage levels. Individual examples are perhaps the best indication and the more they can be quoted, the more complete and reliable the picture becomes. There is however a further difficulty in trying to assess living standards. It's quite clear that many families had several sources of income, not only because households were often extended to include working brothers, fathers etc., who presumably contributed towards expenses, but beacause 141 houses had lodgers paying rent. It has already been noted that at the corner-shopkeeper level of society, the income was often an adjunct to the husband's income and that many 'larger' shopkeepers in Driffield were property owners with an income from rents.It is also noticeable how many individuals, particularly in clerical occupations, had incomes from several sources. The census, whilst obviously an exceptional circumstance, is nevertheless an example of the way in which people with these skills found ways of adding to their income. Such 'diversification' reached all levels of society. James Jennings presumably obtained the bulk of his income from his legal business in Exchange St., but he was paid as the coroner, as the clerk to the magistrates and to the Commissioners of Taxes. He was paid £35 as clerk to the Driffield Navigation and was clerk to the Burial Board. He was the agent of the Conservative M.P., responsible for the registration of people qualified to vote. Perhaps under the circumstances he was unwise to bring up the complaint of jobbery in the Agricultural Society. In a similar way, William Jarratt, the bank manager, was also chairman of the Linseed Oil Company and the proprietor of the cattle market, as well as agent for the Yorkshire Insurance Company.

Clearly great caution needs to be exercised in trying to generalise about either wages, incomes or standards of living. What is clear however is that agricultural workers, particularly married ones, were among the poorest section of employees. This was recognised at the time. In the same leader in which Holderness criticised the poor, "a large proportion of whom are poor from their own faults", he wrote without any apparent sense of contradiction, that "whilst farming flourishes farm labourers, who work the longest hours and at the hardest work, can only earn wages upon which they and their families can barely exist and many of them find only partial employment. All therefore who have the means to remove, either flock to large towns where wages are better and work more readily obtained, or help to swell the yearly exodus to Canada."

Matthew Hewson was typical of the way in which people found it possible to combine several roles. He was a building contractor and raff and timber merchant at River Head, bringing material in by the canal. He also owned the Springfield Brewery at River Head and was paid £70 a year as the Inspector of Navigation by the

Commissioners. Fortunately one of his account books survives for the period beginning November 1871 and gives a clear indication of trade on the canal at this time.

Three firms rented warehouses, or parts of warehouses, beside the canal. Dawson and Witty, the corn merchants, paid £40 and £26 a year and also rented wharf space to berth vessels. Mortimer also had warehouse space for £18 a year and had an application in to build a separate manure warehouse. The canal was thriving. Richard Dawson had written to the Commissioners that an outlay of £2000 was necessary "for the accommodation of their traffic" and the Pure Linseed Cake Company was desperate to have improved facilities. They wanted the Commissioners to build "a stone warehouse with all necessary appliances for getting oil and seed in and out of the sloops". The building must be "specially adapted to the company's needs" and leased to them for 21 years at a proposed rent of £4 per % of the capital outlay of the new warehouse. Jarratt, the chairman of the company, complained publicly about the delay in answering this request, claiming that they had had no reply for 18 months to their application; though it is surprising that he could not have speeded matters up, since another of his roles was Navigation Commissioner. [2] Five other local firms rented berths alongside the canal.

An analysis of Hewson's accounts, shows that 41 different captains berthed at River Head in November, a number of them making several visits. The largest number on any one day was seven vessels. Between them, they transported 2124 tons of goods in the month and paid dues of £60-7s-10d, though it should be remembered that the Navigation had always been perceived as an asset to the town rather than as a profit making body. This was one reason why it was able to withstand the competition of the N.E.Railway. Another reason was the nature of the goods using the canal. The mainstay of the trade was coal, ordered by local coal merchants and by the Gas Company, who rented a berth. Linseed, linseed oil and cake went both to Jarratt's and to Matthews' company, who also received cargoes of manure, as did

Foster at Little Driffield. All the millers brought in coal for their mills and sent cargoes of flour out. These were the everyday cargoes, but Hewson had 22 tons of timber delivered and Taylor 4 tons of mahogany. Sterriker, the chemist, had salt and oil conveyed, whilst Clark, the ironmongers, had 1 ton of Naptha delivered. Bark for the tannery at Little Driffield, bones, pots and ashes, iron for Pickering, all appear in the manifests. The Navigation fixed dues of 2d a ton for wheat, beans, peas, rye, oats, barley, rape seed, maize and malt, but November was not the month for such goods to show up in the accounts. In general terms, the sloops carried about 70 tons in any one voyage and it is clear that the canal was a thriving facility in the town, which the local business community was anxious to see expand and develop.

REFERENCES

1 Woodcock p27
2 H.C.R.O. : DDIN/2 and DDIN/3. Hewson's accounts are in DDIN/5

CHAPTER TWELVE

DECEMBER

The Board of Guardians held their regular fortnightly meetings not at the Workhouse on Nafferton Rd., but in the boardroom of the former workhouse in Middle St.,which was considered to be a more convenient place to meet than on the edge of town. It had been retained when the rest of the workhouse was sold in 1868. The December meetings were not exceptional [1] They noted the punishment of Thomas Prince, a labourer from London, 21 days in the House of Correction for tearing up part of his bed clothes and refusing to do his task work in the workhouse and they confirmed that each able-bodied male over 15 had to break 3 cwts. of stone a day in return for his keep. They decided that . the raised sleeping boards of the female vagrant ward, which had hitherto been in the form of a long bench, should "be divided into partitions of the same height and in the same manner as the male ward". They also decided that baths should be fitted up next to each vagrant ward to allow "a tepid bath and for disinfecting their clothes when necessary".

Mrs Kirby of the Bell, was thanked for the £11-0s-6d that had been collected towards the inmates' Christmas dinner.This was an annual undertaking and the previous year Mrs Kirby had requested that any surplus from the £10 collected should go to the Cottage Hospital fund. Local butchers contributed pork and beef and there was plum pudding. The dining room was "tastefully decorated" with mottoes reading 'Poor but Cared For' and 'Lambs of the Fold'. The dinner was attended by a large number of local worthies, who distributed toys to the children.

The 1834 Poor Law Amendment Act had sought, as a matter of policy, to discourage people from seeking relief by deliberately making conditions inside the workhouse worse than those of the poorest labourer outside. In the early days of the new Act as it operated in Driffield, the overall impression was of a well-meaning if not very imaginative or sensitive group of people, the Guardians, struggling to deal with a centralised bureaucracy, uncertain of their own powers and constantly seeking guidance from the newly created administration.Things had probably changed for the better since 1834, at least in the sense that the Guardians had a better understanding of the tasks they faced, but 'the Grubber' was always there in the lives of the poor and those who entered it lost their status in society. They were to be pitied and a sense of this comes from a report in the Times at the opening of the new workhouse in 1868, situated perhaps a mile away from the old one. "It was a moving scene on Monday afternoon to witness the poor paupers wending their weary way through clouds of dust, under a burning sun, to the local palace recently dedicated to pauperism." [2]

Who were the inmates ? The population varied over the year. Wold Rangers, tramps and passing vagrants were more likely to seek a night's shelter in the winter than in the summer. In April, at the census, there were 18 men, 23 women and 39 children in the workhouse. Twelve of these were mentally handicapped and three were blind. Thirteen of the adults were aged over 60. Of the other women, Asenath Dunn, a 40 year old widow with five children, was presumably unable to cope as a single parent, though in Driffield it would perhaps have beeen more usual for her to have been given outdoor relief. It is possible that she had no home to go to. Other women were like the unmarried Eliza Dixon (25), who had just given birth to her 5 day old daughter and was accompanied into the workhouse by her two other children. Twenty-three of the children appear to have been in the workhouse without any family support. In addition to those in the workhouse, the Guardians gave considerable 'outdoor relief', though this was against the spirit of the 1834 Act.

The local regime was regarded, at least by those

who didn't have to use it, as a liberal one. There is some evidence in support of this, since the Guardians were criticised by a new Poor Law Inspector for being over generous in the allocation of outdoor relief. It was pointed out that the Driffield Union with an area population of 19,000 was spending as much as York with a population of 63,000.He recommended retrenchment. Relief should be for three months only and then only after home visits had been made by the relieving officer. Relations should be compelled to contribute and wherever possible relief should be in the form of loans.[3] Savings could be made within the workhouse if vagrants were given "coarse gowns to sleep in".

The Driffield Times came to the defence of the local Guardians, pointing out that in the case of outdoor relief, a widow with either five or six children would receive 6/- to 8/- a week. It calculated that this meant each member of the family living on 2¼d a day. It praised the Wilsons, the workhouse master and matron, for the liberal attitude with which they ran the institution. "The house which is to be the home of pauper children, the refuge of the destitute sick and the place where the aged poor are to pass the last few weeks or years, should be one not only of cleanliness and decency but of such comfort as circumstances will allow. ..... It would be a sad day when the poor should be content to avail themselves of such shelter save in cases of pressing necessity."

The central Poor Law administrators kept a close eye on the local Guardians. Early in 1871, the Guardians decided by 8 votes to 7 not to replace the chaplain, who resigned on leaving the district. Their decision was immediately questioned. How would consolation and religious instruction be provided ? The Guardians approached the Vicar to provide a weekly service, but he refused. He already gave two services on Sunday and didn't go out at night. The nonconformist ministers would perform a service each week and Anglican paupers would be allowed to go to church. This failed to satisfy the Inspector. Old people would have to walk a mile to church. To take the children would mean extra work for the staff and Anglican children should, under no circumstances, be allowed to attend dissenting services in the workhouse. The Guardians should reconsider their decision. In the end, the Guardians decided to ask the opinion of the paupers as to whether they wanted a chaplain and on learning that they did, they appointed the Rev. Richard Allen, the Vicar of Kirkburn, at £25 a year.

There are signs that within the powers that were available to them, the Driffield Guardians did their best to run the institution in what they regarded as a humane manner. They were conscientious in visiting children hired out to work and in placing Sarah Sellers in a suitable school for the blind. Their own school was regarded as good, the Inspector reporting that the boys "did great credit to themselves and to the schoolmaster" and that in the case of the girls "the schoolmistress deserves great credit for the way she got them on ". The children were taken to Bridlington for the day, paid for by Miss Grimston at a cost of 30/-. All these were positive signs, but the 'palace' would always stand for loss of independence, the separation of families, the relinquishing of personal possessions, the donning of workhouse uniform, the acceptance of workhouse discipline and the last resort for any self-respecting person in 1871.

At the other end of the social scale, the visit of the Prince of Wales to Lord Londesborough, caused much excitement, particularly as the royal party travelled between his lordship's estate on the Wolds and Londesborough Lodge in Scarborough by special train, two saloon carriages and an ordinary first class coach. Unfortunately the royal constitution proved no more resistent to germs than that of anyone else, and Edward contracted enteric fever. He was dangerously ill for much of December and it was a matter of some doubt as to whether he would survive. The Driffield Times had a long leader on the Prince's illness and carried the bulletins of the royal doctors. Several local social events were cancelled as they were seen as inappropriate at such a time. One of these, a Masonic Concert and Ball, drew a letter of protest from 'A Father of a Family', who felt that this was one of the few events to which he was happy to take his family, since "all the Balls I've been to, have been stuck up affairs, designed it seemed to me, for the enjoyment of about a score of what they call the upper classes in the neighbourhood, whose presence was always a check upon people like ourselves". There was widespread rejoicing when "the illustrious patient, whom we have all been watching so intently" recovered before Christmas.

There were few signs of the Christmas spirit in the Driffield Observer on December 9th. The editor had a long running dispute with his neighbour, a Mr Gamble. The cause of the quarrel was trivial in the extreme, but Holderness took the case to court claiming damages and Gamble counter-charged claiming assault. Much to the editor's amazement and annoyance the court found against him. Holderness had his revenge in the next issue, printing a leader headed 'Our appearance in court' that lashed out at everyone concerned, particularly the Magistrates. "We are so unfortunate to live next door to Mr Gamble, who is constantly annoying and insulting us." Gamble's answer was "the most lying case we have ever heard" and "nothing but the grossest perjury". The competence of the J.P.'s was questioned in a tone that must have amounted to contempt. It was clearly wise to beware of offending Victorian newspaper editors.

The Mechanics' Institute had begun its winter programme with a Grand Amateur Concert and had two events programmed for December, a lecture by Dr Britton on 'Traits of Character' and a slide show on 'English and Irish Lakes'. The shops were full of Christmas goods. Turner had a display of Christmas tree ornaments and Mason, who had a nursery at Little Driffield, sold Christmas wreaths, crosses and trees from his flowershop on the corner of Eastgate. Jackson had had his shop refurbished and restocked for the season, with, as in previous years, a splendidly decorated Christmas tree as the highlight of his display. The cattle market had a special auction of fat stock for the Christmas trade, including "10 prime,fat oxen weighing 60-70 stones each" from Neswick, 12 Aberdeenshire bullocks from Nafferton and Shropshire Down, West Down, Border and Leicester sheep.

The Driffield Times set its annual Christmas competition for children, awarding seven prizes in all. They offered a book for the best essay on the 1870 Education Act and a box of dominoes to any boy under eleven, who was desperate enough at Christmas to work out an answer to a problem :- "Suppose Mr Blanchard had a bed of clay, 150 yards long, 90 yards broad and 2 yards deep, how many flooring tiles 9" square and 3" thick can be manufactured out of that bed?."

The Driffield Observer had a leader comparing Christmas past with Christmas present and "frankly we have no regrets for those good old times. There was less of genuine benevolence and kindly charity than in our day." Moreover, "the railway makes travelling so easy and cheap, the saving of time considered, that Christmas family meetings must be more common than ever". Reviewing the year in the time honoured manner of newspapers, he found "the country under far happier conditions than last year. Then two great nations were at war...... we were suffering severely in restricted commerce and depressed trade....... but the Christmas of 1871 finds the country prosperous and happy."

It is perhaps fitting that any account of Driffield in 1871 should end with the topic that had dominated much of the year, education. The Board had made a firm decision in June to reject Jarratt's new schoolroom in Harland Lane "as it does not meet the requirements of the town " and to seek a site for a new school on the eastern side of Driffield. Despite this, the National School managers were still trying to persuade the Board at the end of September, that the voluntary schools were successful, that only a small increase in the number of places was needed and that the extension of the National Schools would minimise the cost to the rates. Jennings was clearly losing patience. He "had a very vivid impression of the state of things when Mr Stead was the master, and the kind of schoolroom that then existed". A formal resolution declared "that the opinion of the ratepayers having been so clearly and decidedly expressed......is a declaration on their part that the system of management in the Driffield National Schools has not been so successful as (the managers) seem to suppose". There was only one dissentient. At the following meeting, Jarratt came with a prepared statement to read in defence of the National managers' position. He attacked Whitaker as unfit to sit on the Board. Whitaker demanded the protection of the chair and "mutual recrimination ensued" before Jennings abandoned the meeting. The Times reported it under the heading "A Scene at the School Board". "Ever since the first meeting of the Board, two powerful and antagonistic elements have been warring against each other .....these two members of the Board, (Jarratt and Whitaker) the chairman has found hard work at times to restrain in their enthusiasm."

The Board advertised for a suitable site of not more than one acre, but it was obvious that it would be a considerable time before the school was built and ready to open. They approached the Wesleyans and the Congregationalists to use their schoolrooms as temporary accommodation at a rent of £26 and £15 a year. Both rooms were fitted with desks that were fixed to the wall and which could be let down against the wall when not in use. These were constructed by Shepherdson at a cost of £15, Jarratt attempted to delay matters by arguing that the Board could not legally spend parish money before the Council of Education had agreed how much accommodation was needed.

Whitaker was delegated to draw up the bye-laws of the new school. These provided for a mixed infants' class and two separate sexed senior classes. Fees were to be kept to a minimum, a 1d a week for infants and 2d a week for seniors. The infant curriculum would be reading, writing, arithmetic, music and drill. The seniors would, in addition, study English grammar and composition, the principles of book-keeping, mensuration (for the boys only), elementary geography, social economy and drawing, the history of England and they would have object lessons in physical science. The girls would have plain needlework and cutting-out lessons. Provision was made for extra lessons for the more advanced in algebra, geometry, physical geography, animal physiology and domestic science. These draft regulations received careful scrutiny, but the most interesting amendment was that the Board decided to ban corporal punishment.

Relationships on the Board were becoming very strained and trivial matters became issues. Thus, instead of using the vast Corn Exchange, Jennings put his office on Exchange St. at the disposal of the Board and the press for their meetings. It was doubtless warmer in winter and more convenient. Jarratt objected and argued that the Board should pay for the use of the room. On another occasion Jarratt demanded to know if it was true that three pianofortes had been bought for the schools. Jennings had difficulty in keeping his patience.

Nothing illustrated the breakdown in relationships more than the appointment of the new master. The Board received twenty-five applications and drew up a shortlist of three, offering the position to E. Swithenbank, a married man of 26 from Mansfield, at a salary of £100 a year. After some prevarication about being released from his present post, Swithenbank withdrew, declining to take office under the code that had been drawn up. "He deprecated severe bodily punishments as much as any member of the Board .... but at the same time he believed a judicious application of the rod was necessary and expedient in arousing the supineness of one class of pupils and quelling the defiant conduct of others." The Board then turned to the second of the short-listed candidates, Sparks from Staffordshire, and offered him the post at £110, "his own proposed salary". Sparks too had his reservations about the punishment code and in the meantime had had a better offer, but would accept the post at £130 a year. The increased demand for teachers after the 1870 Education Act meant that they were in short supply and could command higher salaries for a time.

The Board accepted the new terms and wrote to

113

Sparks inviting him to attend, but the following week, December 7th, Jarratt declared his intention to write to Sparks privately to warn him that the Board was, in his view, exceeding their authority in acting independently of the Council of Education. After a heated discussion in which he was told by Jennings that he was "greatly exceeding his duty", Jarratt "took his hat and wished his brethren good night". Understandably Sparks was more than a little alarmed to receive a letter from a member of the School Board stating that "the great possibility was that no capitation grant could be obtained by the Board ", that the members were "acting entirely on their own responsibility" and had "no authority" from the Council of Education to carry out their proposals. It needed a reassuring letter from the Clerk to the Board before Sparks would confirm his acceptance of the post. At a special meeting on the 14th, the Board passed a resolution condemning Jarratt's behaviour after a blistering attack on him by Jennings. "Was not Mr Jarratt's conduct ever since his election ..... attributable to a secret fear underlying everything - a fear lest these schools so persistently opposed in every possible manner, should prove more acceptable to the working classes than those with which he was officially connected."

Nor was the Board any more fortunate in appointing a mistress. There were only three applicants and the first choice, a Miss Eadington from Belford, turned down the post as the salary of £80 was insufficient. Miss Mary Carter, a 22 year old pupil-teacher at the Borough Rd. School, was then appointed at £60. Both she and Sparks were to commence their duties on January 8th at 9.00 a.m..

In one sense that was the end. Jarratt had tried to delay the Board for as long as he could, but he was unable to prevent the majority achieving their aim. He fired one more broadside, a long letter to the Observer on December 23rd, justifying his actions in writing to Sparks. "The other members of the Board felt so much aggrieved that they devoted an evening to the discussion of my faults, and they satisfactorily ended

their discussion with their usual unanimity." Early in
the new year the Board accepted an offer from the lady
of the manor, Lady Downe, of of an acre of land at the
corner of Wansford Rd. and Nafferton Road. The choice of
site was opposed by the New Rd. householders, who felt
that the school would undermine the value of their
property. In the same week Jarratt resigned as a manager
of the National Schools and the Harland Lane schoolroom
was abandoned.

Perhaps influenced by Jarratt's letter in which
he claimed to have tried to protect "the property of the
already overburthened ratepayers", there was a flurry of
last minute opposition in December. George Hopper, a
shopkeeper in Middle St., tried to win the support of
the major ratepayers to veto the new school in some way,
claiming it would lead to a new rate of 15/- in the £1.
He was successful to the extent that an "influential
committee of principle ratepayers" was set up, committed
to provide voluntary school accommodation in place of a
Board School.

There were two significant replies. The
Driffield Times had a powerful leader on December 30th
attacking Hopper and his supporters. "The means that
have been taken in the town to blind and deceive the
people with regard to the operations of the School Board
are so glaring that we would have supposed that they
would simply suffice to provoke mirth. ..... (It is
claimed)expenses contemplated by the Board would cause a
rate of 14/- in the £1 and numerous signatures have
actually been obtained upon such representation. 1d
or 2d will cover all."

Equally significant was a letter from "A
Working Man" to the Observer on December 23rd. It
deserves quoting in full if only to balance George
Whiting's 'A Fast Town', written a little earlier.
"A Hint to my Fellow Working Men"
*Mr Editor-- I know you sympathise most fully with
the wishes of the working classes. Will you allow me to
say a word to my fellow men. Just a few plain words
which I know they will understand.--- Fellow workmen:-
a number of gentlemen are taking a great interest in us*

just now. They are saying a great deal about us--and some of them become very excited and find it difficult to keep their temper. They all seem to know what we want, and yet if they do know what we want, some of them express it in a queer way. Didn't we show them something at the School Board election that was our victory! It was won by equal voting, for depend upon it if these large ratepayers of whom we hear so much just now , had been allowed to give 6 votes each, no School Board would have been appointed. Now it has struck me that in the midst of all this talk, we might say something for ourselves, We know what we want! Can we not meet somewhere on Christmas day evening in large numbers and get up our requisition ? The Education Bill was for us, surely the Department will listen to us as well as they will to Mr Jarratt. Cannot we tell Mr Jarratt that we never went to the poll for a school in that dirty lane ? That we do not ask for his benevolence ? The Government has given us the opportunity of obtaining our own schools and selecting the managers, and we will not have from private benevolence what we can claim as a right ! These gentlemen don't understand working-men's thoughts about this matter. We would rather pay for our children at a Board School than we would have Mr Jarratt's Free school. We have self-respect as well as others. Fellow working men, take a hint, let us try to borrow a chapel or a school room for Christmas evening and have our say about a matter that concerns us more than any other class.

A Working Man

Perhaps the new year should start with 13 year old Anna Cooper of Church St., who became number one in the admission register of the Girls' Board School. Significantly 48 of the 75 girls admitted that first week transferred from the National Schools. It had been a long struggle before Sparks could open the Log Book of the new school and write "Commenced on Monday my duties as Master of Great Driffield Boys' Board School and admitted 120 scholars". It was Jackson in the Driffield Times on January 6th 1872, who pointed out the significance of the new regime.

ADMISSION.

NAME.	Index number.	DATE.	Age.		RESIDENCE.	Parent's occupation	Means of previous Instruction.	TIME previously under Instruction.		Similar passed.
			Y	M				Y	M	
Cooper	1	72	13	6	Church Street	Farmer	Sun S			
...... Clara	2	72	12	6	Birch Street	Printer	Flat S			
Dawson Annie	3	72	13	5	Peel Gate	Stone Mason	Sunok S			
Featherston J. Ann	4	72	6	6	Bell Hall	Gardener	Flat S			
Armstrong	5	72	11	1	East Gate	Labster	Flat S			
...... Rachel	6	72	4	3	East Gate	Farmer				
Atkinson	7	72	11	4						
Atkinson ...... Kemp	8	72	4	0						
Arnett Anne	9	72	6	0	East Gate	Slaughter				
Arnett Emily	10	72	8	3						
Adamson Lizzie	11	72	6	2	East Gate	Farmer	Sun A my			
Ashman Emma	12	72	8	3	North End	Glover	Flat S			
Pay	13	72	11	6	Civilité Ewart	Burvest				
Baird	14	72	7	0	Dundas Road		Private			
Blackburn	15	72	6	1	Chapel Lane	Saloon				
Brampton May	16	72	4	0	Birch Street	Printer				
Britt Ada	17	72	4	4	Middle Street	Grocer				
......	18	72	6	0						
Baines Eliza	19	72	10		Cromwell Rd	Labrer				
Baird Annie	20	72	11	1	Dundas Road					
Bell Elizth Ann...	21	72	11	3	Cromwell Square	Grocer				
Bell Kate	22	72	6	0	Adelphia Street					

117

"The new schools are the schools of the people, paid for by the people, managed by persons elected by the people and if these persons do not manage them as the people choose, they can dismiss them and elect any others whom they please."

Some people at least moved optimistically into 1872.

REFERENCES
1 H.C.R.O.: PUD/4.12.71
2 Driffield Times : 20-6-1868
3 H.C.R.O. : PUD/13.6.72

CHAPTER THIRTEEN

1871. A POSTSCRIPT

At the end of the year, it is perhaps appropriate to stand back from involvement in the pattern of markets, harvests and hirings in order to look at the community to try to see which groups and which individuals influenced and shaped the way in which the town developed.

In an age where education was limited in its spread across society and where 'knowledge', or perhaps simply 'know how' of what could be done and how it could be achieved, was confined to a relatively small number of people, it is perhaps not surprising to find that the influence of such individuals was great. Solicitors were one group that had this 'know how'. They were prominent in most of the public meetings in the town. This was inevitable when the means of achieving change through a representative body such as the School Board, was only just beginning to emerge. The Vestry was a clumsy body through which to assess public opinion and an even more difficult one through which to effect change. In the absence of an effective town council, a telling letter, such as that from Dr Scotchburn on the water supply, could focus the attention of the town and point it in a particular direction. Someone like Jennings, a decent, intelligent man, clearly respected in the town, could exert considerable influence as an individual. It is difficult to believe, on the evidence of 1871, that if he was strongly in favour of a course of action, that his views would not carry considerable weight. Other individuals, such as Jarratt and Whitaker, without having general support and respect, could still exert considerable influence with sections of the community, either through the strength of their convictions or their powers of patronage.

How far did the struggle over the School Board reflect a religious divide ? Jennings was clearly right when he said in his attack on Jarratt that "there does unquestionably exist in the minds of the parents an objection to the present schools, which no amount of argument on the part of the supporters of those schools can remove".For some the basis of that belief may have been religious, but it is difficult to accept that the majority of parents were concerned that the their children were going to be indoctrinated into the Church of England. The root of the objection was surely political, that the National Schools represented a body over which they had no control or influence. The education was being given to them by a group with whom they felt little affinity. The reluctance to use the schools, alongside the apparent reluctance to use the Cottage Hospital, is perhaps because both were seen as undermining independence by a form of charity. Initially, at least, the School Board could be viewed in a different light. It is surely these political aspirations that are being articulated in the letter from 'A Working Man'. "We will not have from private benevolence what we can claim as a right. These gentlemen do not understand working men's thoughts about this matter. We would rather pay for our children at a Board School than we would have Mr Jarratt's free school".

It is at least arguable that these aspirations found expression through the religious divide. The Church of England in the 19th Century was an hierarchical organisation, with a minimum of lay involvement. The nonconformist groups were more susceptible to lay opinions and organisation and in that way at least they were more democratic. The success of the Primitive Methodists may well be, in part at least, because they offered the working class, one area of their lives over which they could exert full control. "They feel at home there as they do not in the parish church."[1]

Without the right to vote and with no trade union activity in Driffield in 1871, it is difficult to

120

find areas outside the life of the chapels, where ordinary people could exercise these aspirations. The Co-operative Society was perhaps one and the Driffield Provident Society, the last of "one of the many secret societies with which Driffield (once) abounded", was perhaps another. It still had 86 members and £372 in the Post Office Savings Bank, out of which it paid sickness and funeral benefits. Yet it is difficult not to see the Mechanics' Institute for example, as being an organisation in which the working class had very little say. In contrast it has been argued [2] that one of the reasons why the Dame Schools survived even the coming of the School Boards, at least until education became compulsory, was that they were under the effective control of the ordinary people. "They paid fees to the teacher (not always punctually) ...... the teachers were working people like the parents, not socially superior 'educated' persons, and they were prepared to take the children at the times and on the conditions acceptable to a working class family." The struggle over the School Board had a lot more to do with politics than with religion.

The local newspapers had a crucial part to play in relation to public opinion. Apart from preaching, they were one of the few means of reaching an audience. Little can be said of the Driffield Express. The British Newspaper Library has no copy before No 58 for July 1872. At that time it ran to eight pages, twice the size of its two rivals, but it had poor cover of local news and most of the paper consisted of the 'interest' items culled from other papers that all Victorian editors used to fill out their columns.

Thomas Holderness was the town's most experienced journalist, in his eighteenth year as the editor of the Driffield Observer. There is no doubting his professional competence. The paper was well produced, had the best coverage of national and foreign news and, perhaps because it was the longest established paper in the town, tended to get the 'official' adverts. and the weightier letters. Despite Holderness' experience, there has to be a doubt over his judgement on occasions. His 'appearance in court' may be cited in evidence but he apparently felt that the rioters in 1868, who wrecked the Conservative rooms, were paid by the Conservatives to discredit the Liberals.

George Jackson (1838-1893) had learned his trade as an apprentice to Holderness, before leaving him in 1860 to create the Driffield Times and General Advertiser. They had different styles as editors. Where Holderness was content, for the most part, to report, only rarely venturing an opinion, Jackson's touch was both lighter in the reporting and more inclined to adopt an editorial stance. Was he echoing public opinion in the stance or was he shaping it ? Not surprisingly, it would seem to be a mixture of both. It is possible in some issues to see Jackson thinking through a question over several editions of the paper and moving in his opinion on the matter as it becomes clearer in his own mind. Thus his first reaction to the water problem was to reject any idea of corporate action and to put the responsibility on individuals to ensure a pure supply. His attitude changed, perhaps because of Scotchburn's letter, and his subsequent article on the state of the stream must be seen as important in shaping public opinion. He was consistent in taking a reforming stance over the School Board, despite his Anglican beliefs, and he took a strong stand over Hopper's alarmist tactics over the rates. His attitude over the workhouse and the question of outdoor relief was a liberal one. It seems probable that his approach was both beneficial and influential and that Driffield was fortunate to have George Jackson as a newspaper editor in 1871.

REFERENCES

1 Woodcock p88
2 Harrison : The Common People : p291 Fontana

LIST OF TABLES AND APPENDICES

1. Sketch maps of Driffield in 1871
2. Birthplace of Driffield heads of households
3. The age structure of the population in 1871
4. Male occupations in Driffield in 1871
5. Female occupations in Driffield in 1871
6. Women in Driffield aged 16-45.

APPENDIX ONE

SKETCH MAPS OF DRIFFIELD IN 1871

There have been many articles in local papers over the years on the street names of Driffield. Few have identified the period of which they have written and as the street names frequently changed, the issue has become somewhat confused. In the following sketch maps the names in capitals (e.g. NEW ROAD) are the names used in the 1871 census. The names in brackets e.g. (Exchange St) are the alternative names for that street that were also in use in 1871. The census was not concerned with streets on which no one lived and if I have found no contemporary reference elsewhere, I have left the street blank. Thus I would be surprised if Pinkney Lane was not in use as a name in 1871 but I know of no example. On the other hand, one or two names in use in 1871 can not be positively identified. Love Lane, an earlier name for Shady Lane about 1815, seems to have been used for Etherington Lane (or a parallel lane) in 1871. I have not included it.

The sketch maps need to be treated with caution. They are not to scale and I have made no attempt to indicate the relative size of buildings. The census was not concerned with lock-up shops, workshops, warehouses, offices, churches and other such buildings. It is inevitable that the majority of these are missing from the sketches, though some have been included from other sources. Empty building plots and undeveloped land are another obvious problem. Nevertheless, despite the errors which I am sure exist, I believe that the maps do give a reasonable indication of the 'shape' of Driffield in 1871.

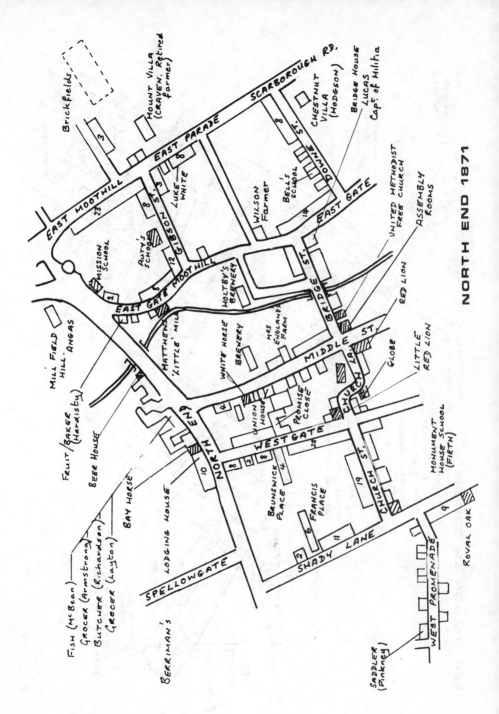

NORTH END 1871

Brickfields

Mount Villa (Craven. Retired farmer)

SCARBOROUGH RD.

Chestnut Villa (Hodgson)

Bridge House Lucas Capt. of Militia

EAST PARADE

3

DOWNE ST.

8

Bell's School

Luke White

8

Wilson Farmer

EAST MOOT HILL

23

GIBSON ST. 3

8

Auty's School

12

EAST GATE

14

UNITED METHODIST FREE CHURCH

ASSEMBLY ROOMS

Mission School

East Gate Moot Hill

Matthews 'Little' Mill

Holtby's Brewery

BRIDGE ST.

RED LION

Mill Field Hill. Angas

White Horse Brewery

Mrs England Farm

MIDDLE ST.

GLOBE

LITTLE RED LION

Fruit/Baker (Hardisty)

Beer House

Union House

Promise Close

CHURCH LA.

Little Red Lion

Monument House School (Firth)

Bay Horse

Lodging House

North End

4

10

WESTGATE

22

CHURCH ST.

Fish (McBean)

Grocer (Armstrong

Butcher (Richardson

Grocer (Layton)

Brunswick Place 4

8

8

Francis Place

19

9

ROYAL OAK

Berriman's

SPELLOWGATE

6

11

SHADY LANE

2

WEST PROMENADE

SADDLER (Pinkney)

125

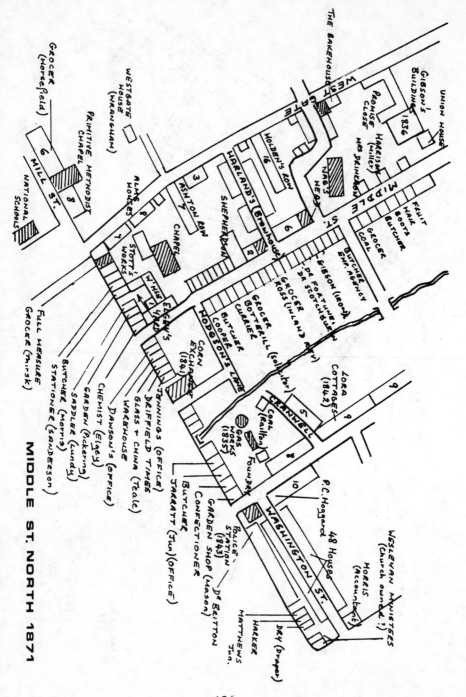

MIDDLE ST. NORTH 1871

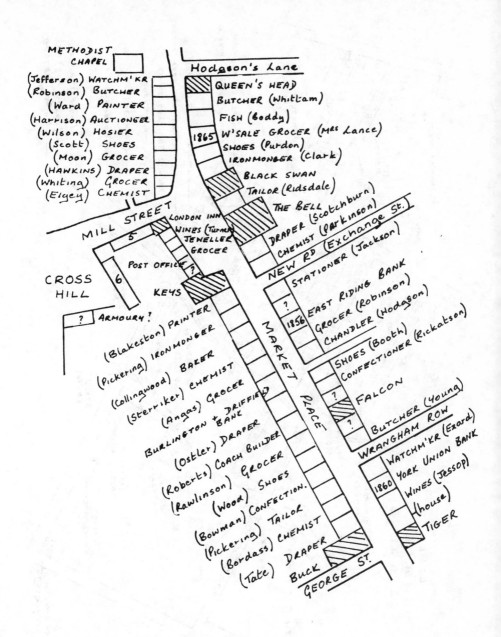

MARKET PLACE 1871

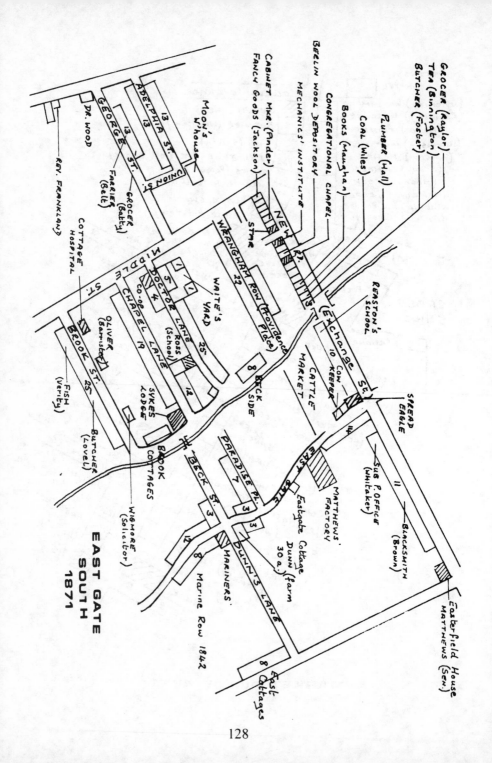

EAST GATE SOUTH 1871

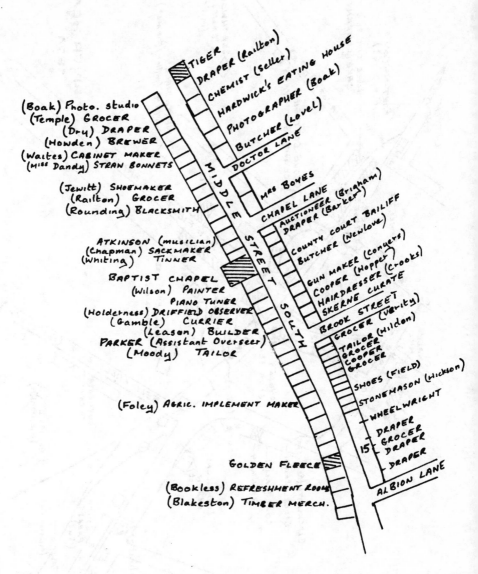

TIGER
DRAPER (Railton)
CHEMIST (Seller)
HARDWICK'S EATING HOUSE
PHOTOGRAPHER (Boak)
BUTCHER (Lovel)
DOCTOR LANE

(Boak) Photo. studio
(Temple) GROCER
(Dry) DRAPER
(Howden) BREWER
(Waites) CABINET MAKER
(Miss Dandy) STRAW BONNETS

(Jewitt) SHOEMAKER
(Railton) GROCER
(Rounding) BLACKSMITH

MIDDLE STREET SOUTH

MRS BOYES
CHAPEL LANE
AUCTIONEER (Brigham)
DRAPER (Barker)
COUNTY COURT BAILIFF
BUTCHER (Newlove)
GUN MAKER (Conyers)
COOPER (Hopper)
HAIRDRESSER (Crooks)
SKERNE CURATE
BROOK STREET
GROCER (Verity)
TAILOR (Hilton)
GROCER
COOPER
GROCER

ATKINSON (musician)
(Chapman) SACKMAKER
(Whiting) TINNER

BAPTIST CHAPEL
(Wilson) PAINTER
PIANO TUNER
(Holderness) DRIFFIELD OBSERVER
(Gamble) CURRIER
(Leason) BUILDER
PARKER (Assistant Overseer)
(Moody) TAILOR

SHOES (Field)
STONEMASON (Hickson)
WHEELWRIGHT
DRAPER
GROCER
DRAPER
DRAPER

15

(Foley) AGRIC. IMPLEMENT MAKER

ALBION LANE

GOLDEN FLEECE

(Bookless) REFRESHMENT ROOMS
(Blakeston) TIMBER MERCH.

MIDDLE ST. SOUTH 1871

129

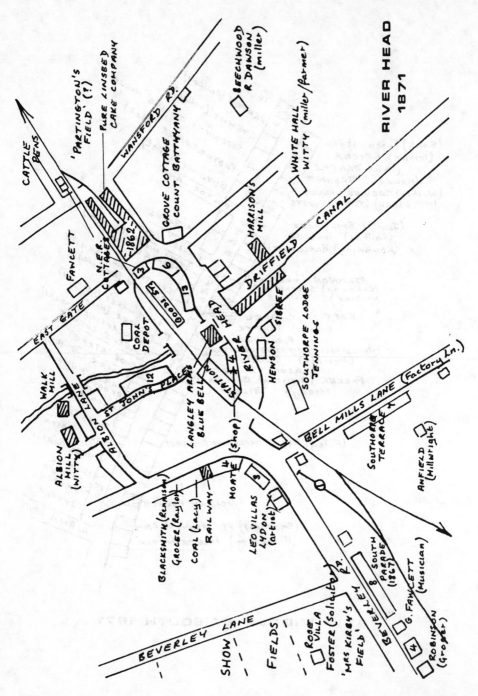

RIVER HEAD
1871

BEECHWOOD
R DAWSON
(miller)

WANSFORD RD.

PURE LINSEED
CAKE COMPANY

'PARTINGTON'S
FIELD' (?)

CATTLE
PENS

GROVE COTTAGE
COUNT BATTHYANY

WHITE HALL
WITTY (miller/farmer)

FAWCETT

1862

N.E.R.
COTTAGES

HARRISON'S
MILL

DRIFFIELD CANAL

EAST GATE

(2)

6

GOODS SHED

13

SOUTHORPE LODGE
JENNINGS

COAL
DEPOT

RIVER HEAD

(10)

HENSON
SIBREE

WALK
MILL

ALBION ST JOHN'S PLACE

STATION

BELL MILLS LANE (Factory Ln.)

ALBION
MILL
(WITTY)

LANE

12

LANGLEY ARMS
BLUE BELL

SOUTHORPE
TERRACE X

ANFIELD
(Millwright)

BLACKSMITH (Renison)
GROCER (Raylor)
COAL (Lacy)
RAILWAY

MOATE (shop)

4

3

LEO VILLAS
LYDON (artist)

SOUTH
PARADE
(1867)

G. FAWCETT
(Musician)

ROSE
VILLA

FOSTER (Solicitor)

'MRS KIRBY'S
FIELD'

BEVERLEY RD.

8

4

ROBINSON
(Grocer)

BEVERLEY LANE

SHOW

FIELDS

APPENDIX TWO

THE BIRTHPLACE OF DRIFFIELD HEADS OF HOUSEHOLDS IN 1871 (MALE AND FEMALE) AND THE WIVES OF MALE HOUSEHOLDERS

	MALE	FEMALE
DRIFFIELD	25.9%	23.8%
EAST RIDING	47.1%	50.2%
N + W.RIDINGS	11.7%	13.1%
LINCOLNSHIRE	4.7%	4.2%
NORFOLK	1.7%	1.2%
REST OF ENGLAND	6.8%	5.3%
SCOT./IRE./WALES	1.7%	1.6%
ABROAD	0.3%	0.7%

APPENDIX THREE

THE AGE STRUCTURE OF THE POPULATION OF DRIFFIELD IN 1871.

AGE	MALES	%	FEMALES	%	TOTAL %
0-14	982	38.6	992	36.7	37.4
15-44	1041	40.9	1147	42.0	41.5
45-59	337	13.2	335	12.2	12.7
60-79	173	6.8	226	8.2	7.6
80+	7	0.2	29	1.0	0.7
TOTALS 5269	2540		2729		

APPENDIX FOUR

MALE OCCUPATIONS IN DRIFFIELD 1871

Many men had more than one occupation and that has involved some subjective assessment in placing them into categories e.g. George Thirsk kept a grocer's shop and was also a Registrar of Marriages and a solicitor's clerk. He appears in the clerical category on the presumption that his wife looked after the shop. John Dunn, timber merchant and farmer of 30 acres, appears under retail rather than in agriculture. The numbers are not such as to distort the percentages involved, though there is room for argument as to which category some occupations should be in.

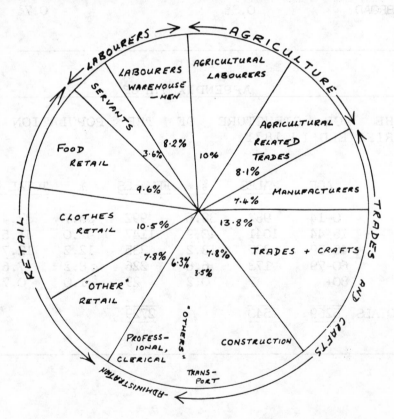

MALE OCCUPATIONS IN DRIFFIELD 1871

GENERAL		SERVANTS		TRANSPORT	
Labourers	118	Coachmen	1	Cartmen	10
Warehousemen	8	Grooms	43	Railway	35
		'Servants'	12	Watermen	9

		AGRICULTURE			
Labourers	153	Cowkeepers	4	Horse d'rs.	5
Machine mfrs.	4	Farmers	15	Pig dealers	3
Bailiffs	5	Fellmongers	5	Poultry d'r	1
Cattle dealers	4	Gardeners	35	Shepherds	14
Corn milling	34				

		MANUFACTURING			
Brick/tile mkr.	15	Linseed wkr.	35	Rope manfr.	1
Coach builders	20	Machinist	1	Sack manfr.	1
Engineers/f'rs.	27	Manure mfrs.	11	Sewing mach.	1

		CONSTRUCTION			
Bricklayers	30	Builders	7	Joiners	72
Plasterers	3				

		TRADES AND CRAFTS			
Basket makers	3	Gas makers	8	Sawyers	15
Blacksmiths	39	Ironmoulders	21	Stonemasons	13
Brush makers	2	Locksmith	1	Tanners	12
Cabinet makers	8	Painters	13	Whitesmiths	13
Clay pipe maker	1	Plumbers	6	Upholsterers	4
Coopers	5	Printers	34	Wood engr'r	1
Curriers	4	Raff merchs.	3	Well sinker	1
Cutlery grinder	1	Saddlers	11	Wood turners	4

		FOOD RETAILERS			
Bacon factors	3	Errand boys	19	'Provisions'	11
Bakers	5	Fishmongers	4	Sausage mfr.	1
Brewers	13	Fruiterers	3	Tallow chand.	4
Confectioners	4	Grocers/Tea	62	Wines+Spirit	2

RETAIL SERVICES

Booksellers	2	Gunmaker	1	Medicine d'r	1
Coal dealers	8	Hairdressers	4	Photog'phers	2
Commercial reps.	8	Ironmongers	7	Public h's	22
Dealers/hawker	20	Jewellers	9	Sweeps	2
Druggist/chem.	17	Marine stores	2	Timber merc.	2

CLOTHES RETAIL

Boot and shoe	59	Drapers	48	Tailors	54

PROFESSIONAL AND ADMINISTRATIVE

Actuary/accountants	3	Doctors	5
Attorney/solicitors	9	Insurance agent	1
Auctioneers	2	Inland Revenue Officer	1
Bank managers	3	Police officers	3
Book keepers	4	Poor Law officials	4
Clerks	27	Post Office workers	8
Company secretary	1	Religious Ministers	11
		School masters	11

APPENDIX FIVE

FEMALE OCCUPATIONS IN DRIFFIELD IN 1871

OCCUPATION	AGE							
	Under 15	15-20	20+	30+	40+	50+	60+	70+
SERVANT	35	108	85	3	5		3	1
CHILD MIND/NURSE	6	5	1	3	5	7	2	1
COOK		2	17	2	4	1		
HOUSEKEEPER			10	5	4	4	2	1
WORKHOUSE MATRON						1		
LAUNDRESS/CHARWN.		1	3	12	9	11	12	3
STAYMAKER				1		1		
DRESS/MILLINER		33	42	23	13	6	3	3
STRAW BONNET MKR.			1	1	2			
BOOK COLOURERS	3	1	3	1				
BOOK BINDER		2	1					
SEWING MACHINIST		3	3					
PUBLICAN					1	4	1	1
BARMAID	2		2	2				
CHAMBERMAID			2			1		
DAIRYMAID		1						
SHOPKEEPER				2	3	2	1	
SHOP ASSISTANT		1	1	1		1		
FLORIST							1	
GLOVER/HOSIER						1	1	
FARMER							1	
BREWER							1	
BRICK+TILE MFR.				1				
REFRESHMENT ROOM						1		
SEED DEALER						1		
WHOLESALE GROCER				1				
GROCER				1				
LODGING HOUSE KPR.						1	2	5
GOVERNESS		3	4					
SCHOOL MISTRESS		2	5	4	3	3	2	1
MUSIC TEACHER	1							
HAWKERS/PEDLARS			1	2	2			
SILK WEAVER				1				

APPENDIX SIX

WOMEN IN DRIFFIELD 1871 : AGE 16—45

NUMBER OF CHILDREN IN MARRIAGE

Age	Unm.	Mar.	Wid.	0	1	2	3	4	5	6	7	8	9	10
16	46	—	—											
17	44	2	—	1	1									
18	37	—	—											
19	38	5	—	2	3									
20	39	9	—	4	1	4								
21	45	6	—	2	2	2								
22	25	21	—	8	8	5								
23	30	14	—	6	4	3	1							
24	16	20	—	3	10	4	3							
25	16	25	—	5	8	5	7							
26	6	34	1	8	9	9	4	4						
27	13	12	1	—	5	5	2							
28	13	23	—	5	5	3	5	3	2					
29	9	28	1	6	5	6	5	6						
30	6	45	3	7	7	10	11	6	3	1				
31	8	28	1	5	3	3	7	5	4	—	1			
32	8	25	1	4	—	5	6	6	—	2	2			
33	4	30	1	3	7	4	5	8	2	1	—			
34	4	15	—	3	3	1	3	2	2	1	—			
35	9	23	2	5	3	4	3	1	3	1	3			
36	4	15	1	2	5	2	—	2	4	—				
37	4	42	3	5	3	12	8	6	4	3	—	—	1	
38	3	19	1	2	2	—	4	4	3	2	2	—	—	
39	5	25	1	3	4	3	4	3	3	3	1	1	—	
40	8	38	5	8	5	2	6	5	5	2	2	2	1	
41	4	22	2	2	4	8	1	1	1	3	2	—	—	
42	5	21	4	4	2	2	3	3	3	3	1	—	—	
43	1	23	1	2	4	6	3	2	2	—	2	2		
44	2	24	—	2	1	4	7	—	—	1	5	3	—	1
45	3	19	—	2	4	2	2	3	4	2	—	—	—	